MANAGEMENT AND LEADERSHIP IN EDUCATION

Series Editors: PETER RIBBINS AND JOHN SAYER

Head of Department

Head of Department

Principles in Practice

ANNE GOLD

Continuum

Wellington House   370 Lexington Avenue
125 Strand   New York
London WC2R 0BB   NY 10017-6550

First published 1998 by Cassell
Reprinted 2000

British Library Cataloguing-in-Publication Data
A catalogue record for this book is available from the British Library.
ISBN 0-304-70160-2 (hardback)
     0-304-70161-0 (paperback)

Typeset by York House Typographic Ltd, London
Printed and bound in Great Britain by Redwood Books, Trowbridge, Wilts.

For Frank Zadik, 1914–1995

Contents

Foreword

It is more important than ever to develop the continuum of management and leadership responsibility in schools. The emphasis on headship in Britain has become almost obsessive, and is reflected in the Teacher and Higher Education Bill now in passage through the Houses of Parliament, where qualifications for headship are becoming statutory before all the attendant issues of control, power and selection are even contemplated or the effects on the profession as a whole considered.

Anne Gold asserts that the Head of Department role is probably the most influential in a well-organized secondary school. It is also, along with other forms of middle management, an essential stage of leadership for those who may later become heads of schools and services. She anticipates the adoption of national qualifications for this stage also, and her book will become the key text for Head of Department training.

The generic nature of much 'middle management' responsibility, whether in secondary, primary or further education, is acknowledged in this book, which can therefore be widely used. On the other hand, middle management in general and 'pastoral' responsibilities in particular have had much recent attention, whereas the particular role of the subject head or co-ordinator can too easily be taken for granted.

This book is written for practitioners in the language used in schools. It puts them in touch with research writing, whilst its main thrust is in developing processes in schools. It derives much from a decade of shared experience in training and consultancy across the full range of school management. It updates previous literature and points ahead, also inviting readers to explore their own future, in deciding whether a Head of Department role is what they want.

Right through the range of practical situations examined there run the questions: why are we doing this, and why this way? What informs our practice? It is professionally inadequate to take thinking, policy and strategies from 'above'. All who exercise real professional responsibility contribute to the translation of principles into practice, and to the review of aims and objectives informed by practical learning and contexts of constant change. The role of Head of Department comes across as an exciting challenge.

John Sayer

How to use this book

John Sayer and I had long discussions and brainstorms, separately and Head of Departmenttogether, to choose a title for this book. The final title represents all parts of the equation of managing in schools – there are many ways of managing, and most of them are 'right' as long as they are based on careful reflection and on well thought-out management principles. The search for a suitable title reflected for me the dilemma for managers in education – are they involved in a practical activity, or a philosophical one?

I know that Heads of Department are hard-working people who probably come home each evening drained and exhausted, worrying about particular people and specific issues to be managed. It would be easy at this safe distance from the 'chalkface' to offer clear and logical solutions to the most common problems for Heads of Department, setting those solutions out strategically in simple steps, so that a reader could reach for the book and find sets of plans to be implemented the following morning.

However, I began by wanting to write a book which would meander lyrically through the ethics, philosophy and current thinking about middle management in secondary schools, flavouring my writing with anecdotes and guidelines, but always leaving actual solutions to the reader. I firmly believed, and still believe, that there are always several solutions to a management problem, and the ultimate choice of solutions is guided by personal values, school ethos and the actual situation to be managed.

I very quickly decided that I should try to write a book which took into account both the principles and the practice of management. So the book is probably crisper than I would have made it originally, and it *does* suggest solutions sometimes, but throughout I try to remind the reader to think about educational philosophy whenever possible.

The 'Suggested Activities' blocks exemplify my dilemma: they are often very functional ways of making sense of the theory and philosophy that surround them. The book can be read with or without these 'Suggested Activities' blocks. They are based on the course activities Beryl Husain and I

Institute of Education. They are usually very practical activities which I have included as a way of illustrating, or making more explicit, some of the discussion preceding or following them. The activities can be done with a team or part of a team – they are often suggestions which contribute to teambuilding – or alone. It is hoped that reading them through by yourself will clarify the points made around them in the text.

Anne Gold

Introduction

The role of Head of Department is the most exciting and probably the most influential position in a well-organized secondary school. At the forefront of knowledge about a specific subject, and as a member of the largest team in the school (that of Heads of Departments), the Head of Department has enormous potential to affect decision-making and to influence the direction of the school. Sometimes that potential can be masked by bureaucracy and administration, and the power to dispense and share knowledge and experience may seem temporarily frustrated. But senior managers know the value of good Heads of Departments, and they usually strive to clear the way for inspiration where possible.

This book is written in recognition of the pivotal nature of a role which combines subject expertise with an ability to bring out that knowledge in other people. Running through it will be explanations and explorations of professionalism, where the Head of Department is seen as the expert who manages the teaching and learning within a subject specialism.

For example, Heads of Department are usually knowledgeable in their subject generally, but also have a much wider responsibility than just a body of subject knowledge. Indeed, they may not be the *most* knowledgeable people in their subject, but they may well be the most knowledgeable people about how to teach it and how to ensure that it is well taught. This may include: developing a set of principles which underpin learning and teaching; sharing that development with the rest of the department; ensuring that the department's aims and principles match those of the school; knowing the legal requirements for learning and teaching the relevant subject; successfully supporting the rest of the department in the learning and teaching; contributing to the direction and educational values of the whole school; and representing the department within and outside the school.

There is no one way of managing a curriculum area, or schools in general. Solutions to management problems must take into account at least social, political and academic contexts, and should be underpinned by a set of values which are ethically informed. Thus professional decision-making about management issues will include reflection, attention to notions of equity, and a recognition of the importance of interpersonal skills in managing with other people.

This book is addressed to people who are Heads of Department in secondary schools, and those who are thinking very seriously about whether they really want to become a Head of Department. Pastoral heads may find much that is useful and relevant to them, but on the whole, they do not manage a large, measured and tested curriculum area, and much more of their work is based on sensitive interpersonal skills, with teachers, parents and young people. They deserve several books to themselves!

There are times when the tone here is intended to be very direct and practical, and other times when philosophical and more general questions are raised about the nature of teaching and managing in secondary schools. Some of the writing addresses theoretical frameworks, and other parts offer practical examples and suggestions. In a sense, this reflects the work of a Head of Department – it is always necessary to combine the practical with the philosophical and to be able to articulate the thinking behind the smallest practical detail.

It is intended that a framework for finding solutions to management problems, and thus the solutions themselves, will become clearer as the book proceeds. The chapters have been planned to address the contexts described above. Thus Chapter 1, 'Your organization and your place in it', explores the relationship between a department and a whole school, taking into account the necessity for an understanding of the issues connected with ethical management in general and in schools in particular. It places the department within the school by exploring the links by which a department can put into practice the aims of a school, and by which the aims of the whole school can be contributed to by a department team. The structural position of 'middle manager' is examined here too, as the way to make clear those links.

Chapter 2, 'Working with people' is, I believe, the most important section for a manager who wishes to work effectively and ethically. It is certainly the longest section in this book. Other people are the greatest resource a manager has to work with, and clear principles about working with other people will affect every interaction however large or small. In other words, every contact, from a quick daily greeting (or not), to an annual appraisal interview gives a message to those with whom a Head of Department works about their worth and about the Head of Department's professionalism.

In this section, there is an emphasis on understanding and working with a team because of the assumption that teamwork is the most productive basis for planning and delivering effective subject teaching. The necessity to balance attention to team, individuals and tasks is explored in detail. Theories of groups and teams are introduced, and the realities of running meetings are connected with those theories. Writing about working with the individual teacher includes looking at delegation, motivation, conflict, working with difficult people and professional development. And the task itself – the learning and teaching of the subject – is introduced in this chapter when referring to the necessity of representing the work of the department to the rest of the school, to parents and governors and to the outside world. It is important to have the humility to learn from and to be influenced by the community in which teachers work.

In Chapter 3, 'Managing resources', there is an introduction to some recent literature about managing resources. There is general guidance about resources and equity and about budgeting and fundraising. But research around resource management in schools shows that each school has its own internal resourcing mechanism. Most important of all is to understand the relevant mechanism in each school and to be prepared to work with it proactively – to know the dates well in advance and to be aware of procedures and paperwork necessary to secure what is needed in order to deliver the learning and teaching in each curriculum area.

Chapter 4, 'Managing the curriculum', links very closely with Chapter 1, but describes and explores the part of the role of Head of Department which has probably developed most in recent years – that of curriculum manager or coordinator. There is an attempt to encourage a sense of expertise and departmental autonomy while keeping clear connections with the direction of the whole school. Heads of Department are encouraged to be quite active in Office for Standards in Education (OFSTED) inspection procedures, and suggestions are made about developing ways of knowing how the curriculum is taught by other members of the department. There is a short introduction to some questions about curriculum evaluation, and there are sections on managing change and on suggestions for reading official documentation.

This book can be regarded as a paean to the role of Head of Department. This job is really tough at times, and even the most committed and effective Heads of Department can find that their sense of direction becomes submerged by difficult and mundane administrative tasks. But in a good school, it is a stimulating and exciting position. The real task is to see administration and bureaucracy as the framework for the implementation of a personal philosophy of education. And the Head of Department has access to a number of teams through which that philosophy can be put into action.

In 1995, the Teacher Training Agency recognized the importance of the people they call 'experts in subject leadership and management' by requiring strategies to be developed for their continuing professional development. Both headship of department and the necessity for proper training for that role were validated by that recognition. In November 1996, a consultation paper on standards and a national professional qualification was sent out for comment. It introduced the National Professional Qualification for Subject Leaders 'based on clear standards for those who have the key role of subject leadership and management in primary and secondary schools'. By the time this book is on sale, the National Professional Qualification for Subject Leaders may well be in place.

I have been fortunate to work in education management development in Europe and in several countries in the British Commonwealth. In some countries school management systems could be likened to a very flattened pyramid – only the headteacher is paid for management responsibility, and for instance in Spain, the headteacher is elected for three years and then goes back into the classroom. In other countries, the hierarchy is very firmly described, and promotion through the system is done in clear steps. This book is deeply embedded in the complicated English education structure, but the issues raised, particularly in Chapter 2, are common to education management everywhere. Indeed, I have used some of the suggested activities in several different European countries.

I have worked with Beryl Husain to develop and run courses for Middle Managers since 1990. She articulates an ethical philosophy of educational management more clearly than anyone else I know. We work together at the Management Development Centre at the Institute of Education, University of London. Our course 'Developing Management for Middle Managers' was originally planned for secondary school teachers only – our own school-teaching experience (fifty years between us) was spent in secondary schools. But we, tentatively at first, decided that Middle Management in education has generic similarities in all institutions, and these far outweigh the differences. And we have been delighted over the years to find that Heads of Department in secondary schools, colleges and special schools have found a great deal in common with curriculum leaders in primary schools. The intensive work they do together on our courses quickly persuades them that they will be enriched by their learning together. I hope that this book will be a way of spreading that excitement at learning and at professional development, further than Bloomsbury!

John Sayer first brought me into this work – I went to interview him for some research I was doing about training for management in education, and he offered me a job doing just that. His deeply principled descriptions of education and its management always enthral me.

I am indebted to Michael Marland who read several drafts of this work, and who made sensitive and vital suggestions for change. He did so with diplomacy and with a thorough knowledge of the whole 'field', which gives him a very special understanding and respect for Heads of Department. I always found our discussions stimulating and I learnt a great deal from talking and arguing with him.

CHAPTER 1

Your organization and your place in it

What is a middle manager?

Many people who become Head of Department find it difficult to acknowledge to themselves or to their colleagues that they are managers. This is because so many teachers mistrust the word 'management' and all that it implies. They are keen to resist what they consider may be the importation of the worst aspects of industry into education. The term 'middle management' is unappealing to the same people because it threatens to bring with it ideas about systems, structures and procedures which appear to deny the pain, feelings, discomfort, pleasure and creativity which are intrinsic parts of effective learning and teaching.

It is important to examine some of these doubts. A Head of Department is usually someone who is in a position of curriculum leadership. This may be because of:

- seniority or status
- subject knowledge
- energy
- particular interpersonal or teaching skills
- a clear vision about the teaching of their subject
- a strong commitment to developing students' views of the world through the specific discipline of a particular subject
- a particular understanding of the way organizations work and an ability to work within them (the micropolitics)
- the ability to effect change
- or a combination of these and other reasons.

Suggested Activity 1

If you are a Head of Department, or would like to be one, ask yourself why you got the job, or why someone might select you for it? In other words, what special attributes do you bring to the job? Is your belief about the importance of the learning and the teaching of your particular curriculum area very strong? Are you so committed to exploring your subject and the teaching of it that you enjoy working with other teachers in order to develop strategies to do so?

Heads of Department, particularly as middle managers, are at a peculiarly interesting junction in the map of a school. They are curriculum leaders who are usually at the forefront of knowledge in the study, teaching, evaluation and planning for learning about their particular subject area. Indeed, they are often more knowledgeable about their curriculum area than their more senior teachers who may have been Heads of Department before they were promoted. A Head of Maths, for example, or a Head of Modern Languages, or a Head of Learning Support will probably be more up to date in these fields of learning and teaching than anyone else in the school. It is their responsibility to work with the other teachers in their department to ensure that the school's philosophy of education is interpreted through their particular discipline. And at the same time, they are responsible for fitting their discipline into the general school view.

In this way the whole-school curriculum, or general school view, that they have helped to inform, including such areas as language, aesthetic understanding, or technology, will be delivered through their subject, and will thus link up the school's general philosophy of education.

It is easy to underestimate the power of the constituency of the group of Heads of Departments. This is where decisions about such issues as equitable distribution of resources, the delivery of cross-curricular strands, and the framing of whole-school responses to problems are often negotiated or put into practice. (See Suggested Activity 2.)

This can be a very uncomfortable and ill-defined position within a school. John Sayer uses the image of the sandglass which might be opened up, to show the position of the middle manager in many schools:

> There is that narrow filter between the teaching–learning life of a school and the running of the organisation, a frequently blocked channel which many would wish to see freed and broadened. The trickle between the two parts of the sandglass depends very much on those whose job is in both parts: the team leaders responsible for an area of the curricular programme and at the same time expected by their fellow teachers to secure in the organisation an adequate framework and resource for them to do their work.

(Sayer, 1989, p. 107)

Suggested Activity 2

1   Draw a very simple diagram of your school and your place in it. Locate the teachers and support staff *who work to you*, directly or indirectly, on the diagram. You have management responsibility for these people. This sometimes becomes complicated by the pastoral organization of the school, in which for example Heads of Department are form tutors, or by those more senior teachers whose teaching falls into departmental areas.

2   Then locate the teachers *to whom you are responsible*. These may be the people with whom you will negotiate departmental resourcing, and with whom you develop whole-school responses and strategies. They share out resources among you and other curriculum leaders; you feed back departmental and individual responses. You offer a two-way channel, or information system, which is at the very centre of well-run schools.

3   The third group to locate is the *other Heads of Department or their equivalent*. In some schools, these are seen as the competition or even the opposition – they are the people with whom the limited supply of resources must be shared, sometimes apparently unfairly. In other schools, they are a valuable community – a mutual support group where important ideas about the school are developed and agreed. A well-managed school will encourage debate within this particular community of teachers – they are the curriculum experts. They are usually a large group of thoughtful and enterprising people who have responsibility to manage members of their departments; they are spokespeople for them 'upwards' when working with the Senior Management Team; and they make supporting and non-competitive links across other departments. In this way, they are Middle Managers.

The very nature of the middle management role itself is not always clearly defined, especially in very small departments. There is a tension between having the ultimate responsibility for the planning and delivery of a particular subject or discipline, and having to fit that discipline into a whole school ethos, whilst at the same time contributing to the development of that ethos. The tension is sometimes compounded when the nature of leadership has not been clarified – are Heads of Department to speak for those for whom they have management responsibility, are they to encourage consensus among them, or are they to empower them to speak out for themselves in whole-school meetings?

Indeed, clarity about the locus of management responsibility may be further complicated in schools where curriculum leaders are members of faculties, and are in turn managed by teachers who have overall responsibility for several curriculum areas. In such schools, Heads of Faculty may be middle managers or senior managers – their responsibility may be to help other middle managers with similar subject focuses to make curriculum decisions, or they may be acting as direct conduits to the Senior Management Team.

The exercise of drawing a diagram of the school and the place of middle managers within it may help to clarify the role, or it may show that it needs to be clarified within the school. It is hoped that in describing the structural position of middle managers in schools, some doubts about teachers as managers have been resolved. Chapter 2 will develop the activities of working with people in much greater detail, but first it is necessary to address a very basic question: 'What is management in schools?'

What is management in schools?

If the basic activity of schools is learning and teaching, the basic activity of a manager in a school is to enable other teachers to work as effectively as possible to plan and deliver that learning and teaching. Management is a neutral activity – it is about making something happen. *How* that activity is performed is what makes it acceptable or not – it is not management in itself that distresses teachers so often, but the way that the managing is done.

A school is a group of people, children and adults, who are legally bound together for the purposes of learning and teaching. Whatever the size of that group, in order for that learning and teaching to happen in a useful and constructive way, some people must take some responsibility for ensuring that the others are resourced, supported and enabled to work as well as possible. This is management. Enabling and facilitative management models important and ethical social interactions. As young people learn by example and experience, their witness of and access to empowering management will necessarily help form their own style of interaction with other people. If they see teachers respectfully supporting each other, they will feel themselves to be part of a supporting community, and will learn to support each other as a matter of course.

Some teachers hold very strong views of education as empowering and developing young people, and they place themselves in relation to children as facilitators, not as authority figures. Some teachers think the only real work in schools is done in the classroom with learners, and not with other adults. Both these sets of teachers have something important to offer to the young people they teach, and a good manager encourages and supports their work. The very activity that encourages and supports them is that of management. It follows that management will only be 'done' by people who want to work with other teachers to support the learning and teaching in the school, by people who are happy to interact as readily with adults as with young people. (See Suggested Activity 3.)

> **Suggested Activity 3**
>
> If teaching and working directly with children is still your first priority, ask yourself whether you should be a manager at all. And do not feel that there is something wrong with you if the answer is 'No'.

What is ethical management in schools?

Ethical management is that which is underpinned by a set of clearly articulated principles. A Head of Department who manages ethically will have thought carefully about:

- What does it mean to be educated?
- What power balances are there within society at present and how do they determine the access of young people from different experiences to education?
- Which direction would they like future society (and the young people with whom they work) to take?
- How does education fit into society?
- Does education and learning cease on entry to adulthood?
- How can values such as honesty and awareness of others be modelled?
- What effect does their power and influence have on other professionals?
- How do both adults and young people learn?

These values and the resulting management decisions must fit within the framework of the aims of the whole school. Mike Bottery has taken up some of these themes in his book about the ethics of educational management. He says that the following questions should be asked by ethical school managers about their management activity:

- Does the management of the school promote personal growth?
- Does it treat people as ends in themselves or as means to ends?
- Does it foster a rationality which is not only tolerant of criticism, but actually sees it as an essential part of school and society?
- Does it repudiate the view of human beings as resources to be manipulated, and instead see them as resourceful human beings?
- Does it create an ethos where measures of democracy can be introduced to be replicated within the society at large?
- Does it foster an appreciation of the place of individuals as citizens within their own communities, states and the world?

(Bottery, 1992, pp. 5–6)

Answers to both these sets of questions will affect the way departments are managed. The first questions are about basic philosophical understandings of education and its place in society. Many schools articulate these understandings in the school philosophy that they write publicly in their handbooks. They often include such phrases as: 'encouraging students to achieve their full potential'; 'equality of opportunity'; 'lifelong learners'; and 'taking a constructive place in society'. These ideas are far more complex than the Collins dictionary definition of education as 'imparting knowledge'.

Mike Bottery's set of questions may be read as suggestions for putting the school's philosophy into practice. For example, most schools declare that education is partly about encouraging students to achieve their full potential; thus it is to be expected that the management of schools will work in such a way as to promote personal and professional development. This will be apparent not only in the way the curriculum is planned and delivered, but also within the whole ethos of the school. And this will be one of the underlying principles which would inform the curriculum area planning carried out by Heads of Department. It would, for example, influence the way they and their department talk to young people and to each other, and it would inform the decision-making processes employed together and with students. (See Suggested Activity 4.)

Suggested Activity 4

Here are some questions in order to look at teachers' and head-teachers' perceptions of school 'ethos'. You might ask members of your department to answer the questions by themselves, then compare the answers as a whole team.

The scoring is: 5 = strongly agree, 4 = agree,
3 = don't know,
2 = disagree, 1 = strongly disagree

How would your school score?

In my school   *Score*

Teachers give pupils the confidence to learn.   ☐

Pupils play an active part in the life of the school.   ☐

Good pastoral support is provided for pupils.   ☐

There is a relaxed but purposeful working atmosphere.   ☐

Staff and pupils feel safe and secure.   ☐

Most pupils feel a sense of achievement.   ☐

Teachers have high expectations of pupil behaviour.   ☐

Teachers have high expectations of pupil achievement.   ☐

The buildings and grounds are well maintained.   ☐

Source: Bolam, McMahon, Pocklington and Weindling (1993) *Effective Management in Schools*, p. 9

It is important not to see questions about values and ethics as too clear cut and simplistic. There are always ethical dilemmas for managers. People do not share the same morality or values in minute detail, and the tensions induced by attempts to reconcile values and morality cannot be underestimated. A simple example is about definitions of honesty and of loyalty. Each of these concepts are on sliding scales, and both of them are values to be encouraged in young people through example. (See Suggested Activity 5.)

Suggested Activity 5

You may wish to explore the following dilemmas with other Heads of Department, or with colleagues who hold the same position as you in other schools.

As a Head of Department, how do you show loyalty to members of your team, and yet honesty to those who manage you? In other words – when do you talk to a Deputy Head about the persistent lateness, or habitual unpreparedness, or lack of paperwork of a member of your department? To what extent do you agree with parents and young people or collude with colleagues, when the former produce well-founded accusations about the unprofessionalism of the latter?

How do you translate the school aims into departmental aims?

Schools are expected to make public their values and beliefs about education in their statement about the purpose of their school. This is the brief statement which usually precedes a school's published aims, and which seeks to encapsulate a school's philosophy of education. It is sometimes called a mission statement, but educators are increasingly uncomfortable with this phrase because of its connotations of imposition, of imperialism and of religious connections.

A philosophy of education which really is embedded into the life of a school, which lives and which is recognizable to all who enter the building or who even just read about the school, will take some time to develop. It is a communal activity. Ideally, all those who have a stake in the school – the staff, governors, parents, students and local community – will have the opportunity to contribute to its articulation. Heads of Department, because of their location at the middle management junction of the school, have a particularly important task. As representatives of other teachers and learners, they can ensure that those they represent have a real possibility of shaping the outcome of the exercise. They also have the responsibility, after the agreement of the philosophy of education, of embedding it in their curriculum area.

I would like to explore a little more why it is essential that departmental aims and objectives fit school aims and objectives. The reality is often that the dislocation between personal and institutional aims and objectives, causes stress, depression and disaffection among both teachers and learners. Clearly, the difference between overwork and stress is that the latter is often the outcome of imposed actions to which staff are philosophically opposed. Basic beliefs are challenged, and there is a mismatch between core values and expected activity.

good activity! //

Suggested Activity 6

(You may find that this activity is probably best completed by a whole curriculum area team, maybe during a staff development session)

1   In two sentences and by yourself, without referring to any school literature at this stage, sum up the core purpose of your organization, i.e. the basic philosophy of the school. *(This might take about 10 minutes)*

2   Check with someone that the sentences make sense. *(Allow about 5 minutes each)*

3   Write each set of sentences on a piece of flipchart paper, and post them around the room. *(5 minutes)*

4   Walk around and look at all the sentences. What do they have in common? What are the similarities? How might these ideas be connected with ideas about curriculum? *(15 minutes)*

5   Flipchart a brainstorm of what constitutes the 'Curriculum' (overt, hidden, received, intended, methodology, pastoral, PSHE, etc.) *(5 minutes)*

6   Now attempt to come to an agreement as a group on two sentences to summarize the core purpose of the school. Write the agreed sentences on a sheet of flipchart paper, and post them up. *(15 minutes)*

7   Write up to six principles which underlie the *overall curriculum* of your organization – those six principles should relate to the core purpose of your school. *(15 minutes if working alone, 30 minutes as a group)*

8   Check that the two original sentences and the six principles make sense. Ask the following questions:

   Are they congruent?

   Do they fit?

   Do the sentences lead into the principles? *(10 – 20 minutes)*

9   After checking, copy your 'principles' on to a piece of flipchart paper, and pin it up underneath your sentences of core purpose. *(5 minutes)*

10   Establish up to six *basic* principles which (should) underlie *your particular curriculum responsibility*. Write them on a sheet of A4 paper. *(20 minutes if alone, 35 minutes if working with a group)*

11   Check that those curriculum principles match your organizational principles.

A less extreme reaction is the cynicism which greets us here at the Management Development Centre when we suggest that participants on our courses write down their own and their institution's philosophy of education. There is often a sense of emptiness, insincerity and instrumentality as an initial reaction to our request. However, as we complete Suggested Activity 6, it becomes clear that it *is* possible to put statements of educational philosophy into practice. Indeed, it is a logical process which may seem complicated until it has been worked through, following the stages in which it is written.

When this activity is used as a strategy to link the principles underlying specific areas of curriculum responsibility with those of the whole school, by this stage a set of basic principles will have been developed which are in fact departmental aims.

Suggested Activity 6 (continued)

To check this, ask yourself and your team the following questions:
- Would it be possible to develop your curriculum objectives from the set of principles you have framed?
- If not, would it be easy to adapt the principles?
- Do they match the aims of your institution?
- Who has access to the aims of your institution?
- Did you or your 'representatives' take part in formulating the aims?

The next activity, leading on from this stage, is to develop objectives and success criteria, linking the curriculum principles into the specific learning plans for your department. Further strategies for this activity are suggested in Chapter 4, 'Managing the curriculum'.

Contributing to the development of the priorities of the school

It might seem that the phrases 'middle manager' and 'Head of Department' have been employed interchangeably till now. They are not really interchangeable, except that they share John Sayer's graphic description of the sandglass. It is necessary to look very carefully at that notion of being in the middle and managing upwards, downwards and across. Managing 'downwards' is a somewhat restrictive and inappropriate model. It does not release the energy of creativity that managing upwards allows for, and it makes it too easy to separate off and insulate the different layers of a school hierarchy. It is here that good school managers might link their philosophy of education with their philosophy of educational management, by making sure that communication flows freely and in all directions between different sections of the school.

In other words, if a manager believes in encouraging people to reach their full potential (as learners *and* teachers), then they will want to hear the suggestions those they manage might have for improving the learning and teaching in their curriculum area. There are clearly often ambivalent feelings here: the most effective new teachers must soon learn to steer carefully between making overt and raw criticism of the work done by their colleagues, and freedom to make suggestions about exciting pedagogic innovations learnt during their teacher education. The care with which new ideas are introduced is necessary because schools are so often repositories of habit and tradition. New teachers, whether senior or just beginning their careers, often make suggestions which are greeted with: 'We don't do it like that here'.

A very important task for a Head of Department, therefore, is that of encouraging new ideas, but adopting them in such a way that the members of the department do not feel that their previous activities lack worth and integrity. Indeed, the middle management role also brings with it a responsibility to encourage everyone to contribute ideas and show commitment to the whole school.

Good ideas may be disseminated beyond the confines of a department. A well-organized school where creative suggestions are valued and explored, will be organized in such a way as to give permission to this creativity. This might mean that all teachers feel free to join in whole-staff discussions about policy and practice in the school, or it could mean that staff members trust their heads of department to represent them and their ideas in smaller and more selective planning meetings.

Another location for tension for an effective Head of Department is between championing their own curriculum area outside the department, helping to balance it with other equally important departments, and importing the whole-school plan back into the department. This means that it is sometimes important to raise their sights above the horizon of their own subject to the broader whole-school horizon. And sometimes it is necessary to encourage the whole school to understand how the discipline of a particular subject affects and supports the whole school.

CHAPTER 2

Working with people

Acknowledging power balances

In the previous section I wrote about ethical management and about how an understanding of the power balances in society might explain differential access to education. I also wrote that Heads of Department who have a professional approach to managing with people will have reached an understanding about society which will inform all their personal and professional interactions. I would like to explain what I mean by power balances and access to power, because this understanding is fundamental to any work which involves working with other people and helping them to develop.

Suggested Activity 7

At a very simple level, there is an exercise you could do with members of your department which might begin to explain the above statements. The level of trust among members of your department will determine the success of the exercise. It is also important to remember that autobiography (which this exercise entails) changes depending on the audience. However, as an activity to begin a staff development session this can be fun, and as a way of trying to understand people's perceptions about their own access to power, it can be very helpful.

1   Sit in a circle, in comfortable seats, where everyone can see each other.
2   Go round the circle, taking it in turns for people to say why they came into teaching. If *you* begin the exercise, you can set the tone of the responses.
3   Then ask people to think, privately, about their philosophy of education.
4   Begin a discussion about the linkage between people's entry into work in education and their philosophy of education.

Teachers often come on our courses with the following answers to why they came into teaching:

- I don't know, I always wanted to be a teacher.
- I used to line up my dolls and teach them, from when I first knew anything about schools.
- I had two brilliant teachers who changed my understanding of the world, and I wanted to do that for other people.
- I was unhappy at school, and wanted to try to make things better for other children in the future.
- I love children.
- I love my subject and wanted to spread that love to other people.
- Short working day, holidays, and money.
- Everyone told me it was a good job for women because of the holidays coinciding with your own children's holidays, and because it would also make me a more understanding mother.
- I did other things first, but I wanted a job which entailed working with people.
- I saw becoming a teacher as a way of changing society.
- My father suggested it.
- There are a lot of teachers in my family.
- I had a lot of younger brothers and sisters, so I always spent a lot of time with younger people.
- I was the first person in my family or community to go on to higher education, and I felt that I ought to give my community something back.

An analysis of these responses shows that they fall into different categories which describe the comfort, excitement, awakening, pain, distress, or anger felt in the respondents' own school days. It is possible to understand a great deal about the childhoods, as well as the schooling, of the people who gave these answers. The issues raised here are:

- educating is an activity which is central to social change;
- teaching is sometimes seen to be very like mothering, so women must automatically be good at it;
- teaching is thought to fit in well with parenting which is also women's work;
- personal interaction is essential to a satisfying job;
- the effects of contact with the role model of a 'good' teacher are powerful and lasting;
- education is an agent of change which is accepted by society – it is not seen as subversive;
- family expectations often ensure a choice made to please other people rather than really free choice;
- teaching can be a way of appeasing a social conscience.

And these issues are dependent on whether these teachers felt that they grew up as powerful and articulate members of their society and family, or whether they had no freedom in their choice of career. Those who had good experiences of school and who felt empowered by their teachers wish to have the same effects on those they teach. If they believed that they were listened to in school, if they thought they were appreciated and encouraged by those who taught them, then they want to help children to feel like that. They described education as a way of empowering learners to take part in their own development. They found their own education to be enjoyable, exciting and effective. 'Effective' here means that they felt able to speak up, to understand and challenge what society expected from them, to make decisions about what they expected from society, and to feel strong enough to take the place *they* would like to take in society. Having reached this understanding of society, they want to help children to get there too. There is a sense not only of feeling powerful, but of encouraging other people to feel and understand the same power.

There are other teachers whose educational experiences made them feel powerless – their experience of the education system often made them feel like failures. They appeared not to understand how to operate in school successfully, and they struggled with a sense of inadequacy. Fortunately, though, at some stage in their lives, something happened which allowed them to see that this sense of powerlessness was socially constructed. In other words, they seemed personally to fail, but they understood that the failure was a result of their position in society – it was structural. So although they might continue to feel as if they were failing, they found a way through the education system to gather the higher education certification necessary for a career in teaching. These are people who often attend higher education part-time or later in life than many others, having spent longer gathering entrance requirements than more obviously successful learners.

Research over many years has shown that people from ethnic minorities in Britain, people from working-class backgrounds and the majority of women are not as likely as white middle-class men to be at ease and comfortable with the dominant values of white middle-class British society. This is as true in education as in other parts of our society. Because originally, the British education system was developed for wealthy upper-class males, many of the values which informed decisions about education policy have remained those of wealthy middle-class males. It is sometimes difficult to begin to address these issues with colleagues. However, they are important, and they are the unconscious basis for many decisions in education. These are the values which in particular affect entrance to university and which are used to frame academic success. (See Suggested Activity 8.)

Suggested Activity 8

In a group discussion, address the following questions:

- Which subjects are most valued by academically successful young people and their communities?
- What official and unofficial hierarchies of merit are growing up around the different examination systems?
- Which option choices are made by young people from different sections of society?
- What are society's different expectations of young people because of their family backgrounds?

Much has been written about historical and sociological explanations of the educational positioning of young people from different backgrounds. Paul Willis's (1977) *Learning to Labour* and Bowles and Gintis's (1976) *Schooling in Capitalist America* are both classical texts which still offer good explanations for those who wish to explore these issues further.

It was only in the late nineteenth century that universal education was introduced in Britain. Then it was as a result of fears that the working classes were out of control and unwilling or unable to provide the necessary personpower for the armed forces or for factories, when needed. A universal elementary education system was developed – some sociologists theorize that this system was introduced to make sure that working-class children would be taught to know their place, and would grow into the adults that the industrial society of late nineteenth century Britain needed. The working class was to be controlled by an education system which kept them in their place and which trained them to be obedient rather than questioning. Charles Dickens (1854) gives a graphic account of this sort of education when he describes Mr Gradgrind's model school in *Hard Times*.

The curriculum developed for the elementary education of working-class children changed remarkably little between the beginning of this century and the early 1990s. It is interesting to note that the grouping into subjects of the knowledge which is held to be important for an 'educated' life has changed very little in over ninety years. And elementary school children were offered a very diluted version of the grammar school curriculum.

I have dwelt on the British education system and its hierarchical nature because I wish to explain how notions of power, and access to it, are still important when decisions are made about what constitutes important knowledge and what counts as success and failure in our education system. There can be no surprise that education in general, and the curriculum and examination systems in particular are seen as so politically significant. Power will always lie with those people who appear to understand what is needed in order to benefit from the prescribed curriculum, and who are able to pass mainstream examinations in order to show academic success.

An understanding of the centrality of power is enormously important to a manager in schools. If people are from a section of society which is expected to take decisions, then as learners they will be encouraged to feel powerful about taking their dominant place in society, about making suggestions, about arguing for their beliefs and about challenging the status quo. Those people whose place in society is to be obedient and to accept authority will not usually be taught to challenge. Sadly, though, many people have not realized that their access to power and to certain types of education is dependent on their social position.

The most commanding way of understanding whether we have access to power or whether our way is barred from power and relevant knowledge is to look at writing about 'discourses'. Stephen Ball explains 'discourses' in the following way:

> Discourses are about what can be said and thought, but also about who can speak, when, and with what authority. Discourses embody meaning and social relationships, they constitute both subjectivity and power relations .... Thus the possibilities for meaning and for definition, are pre-empted through the social and institutional position held by those who use them.
>
> (Ball, 1990, p. 2)

A very simple example of discourse in practice is the quick daily greeting that occurs in all organizations at the beginning of a working day. The actual wording of the greeting is probably the least important part of it. The real message it gives to the receiver is encased in:

- whether it happens
- where it happens
- whether it is accompanied by a smile
- whether eye contact is made
- who initiates it
- the tone of voice employed.

It would be helpful here to think about the way the usual daily greetings are given and received. For many people, often unconsciously, these greetings set the tone for their day. They have a far greater effect on a sense of well-being or lack of it, than the actual time and energy expended in the first place. This is because in a very basic way, greetings include or exclude people from shared activity; by the discourse described by the bullet points above, they fine tune the exact placing of the receiver in the hierarchy of the organization.

So when we think again about the responses to the question about entry into the teaching profession, we can see that it might be possible to work out what those teachers had been allowed to feel about their access to power during their own education. They may or may not have difficulty entering into the dominant discourse of white middle-class male education systems. This will be apparent in:

- the way they take part in team meetings

- their expectations of the young people with whom they work
- how they use their membership of the curriculum team
- their relationship with the head of the department
- their attitude to the authority figures in the school
- their attitude to those over whom they have authority.

Working with teams

The interactions of Heads of Department with their team will be influenced by their chosen management style. For example, they may believe that their management style should be one which encourages everyone in their team to take part in decision-making, one which contributes to the development of all the people with whom they work to their highest professional ability, and one which recognizes differences as enriching rather than dividing a team. If this is so, their relationship with their team will be underpinned by two main principles. These will be:

1   That teams are most productive when they are made up of people with different ways of thinking. The differences make for creative energy and enable the team to achieve more for the learning and teaching in your curriculum area than any individual member could by themselves.
2   Everyone in the team should have a voice and be encouraged to use it.

The notion of a department working as a team is probably newer than the notion of a Head of Department as a leader of the learning and teaching in a curriculum area. And it is not an unproblematic notion. Indeed to ignore the problems and difficulties which arise when working with a team would lead to cynicism and a sense of failure because several uncomfortable feelings would be left unacknowledged. Unacknowledged (and therefore 'outlawed') feelings have a way of surfacing as sabotage. It is necessary as a manager to find ways of allowing them to be recognized. (See Suggested Activity 9.)

Suggested Activity 9

One way of beginning the discussion, with other Heads of Department, with members of your own team, or even thinking just by yourself, might be to have the following brainstorm.

Set up two flipcharts, and write the following phrases: one on one chart, one on the other.

The problematic aspects of teams	**The positive aspects of teams**

Then have a brainstorm with the group with whom you are exploring the notion of teams, asking them to tell you which flipchart to put it on when they call out their suggestions.

When we do this brainstorm with our courses, we find that people first put up what they think of as negative aspects, such as competition, conflict, taking too much time, the mediocrity of consensus, and so on. But then, they go on to explore the more positive aspects, and end up by having more positive than negative aspects brainstormed. And this is indicative of much of this sort of work: when teachers are asked about their feelings about management issues, they often begin with their negative feelings which are much nearer the surface, and then go on to the positive feelings which are deeper, more constructive, and often more numerous. The problem is that negative fears are nearer the surface and seem to block the good feelings, because fear is such a strong feeling.

The importance of carefully developed principles cannot be stressed enough. They underpin and inform all decisions, interactions and planning. Take, for example, the first principle – that of welcoming difference. There are many occasions when managing with a team would be easier if everybody in the team was a clone of each other. Leading a team where everyone thought the same way, always agreed, and shared exactly the same discourse of educational values might seem very attractive. Perhaps managing with people would be easier if one allowed oneself to react and to rely solely on intuition, without recourse to reflection or to an ethical framework. But this would not make for development, for a sense of integrity, or for the real excitement that creative work brings.

Gerald Grace (1995) in *School Leadership: Beyond Educational Management* found that on the whole women managers took teamwork 'to be a normal, organic process whereas men referred to "their" creation of teamwork as an important innovation in the culture of the school' (p. 183). Valerie Hall, in her wonderfully named (and written) book *Dancing on the Ceiling: A Study of Women Managers in Education*, published in 1996, explains Grace's findings by her own research. She found that:

> women include their preference for shared rather than unilateral power (there are, of course exceptions), for communion rather than competition, and for support in the potentially isolating position of being a senior manager.
>
> (p. 171)

In the 1980s, many education authorities introduced equal opportunities selection procedures. Before then, many recruitment procedures were dependent on the equivalent of the 'old boys' network' and various other types of micropolitical activities. In other words, the definition of 'the best person for the job', or the most meritorious, was often 'someone who fits' – either a replica of the departing postholder or someone who would adapt to the team without causing any disturbance.

Brainstorming is a technique that is often suggested in this book, because it helps to unlock creativity. But it is rarely done correctly, so people stop using it, or overuse it. Here are some ways of making brainstorming more effective:

Brainstorming

Brainstorming is a way of generating lots of ideas very quickly. It can act as an ice-breaker, it promotes creative thinking, it helps a group of people to focus their ideas for a discussion, and it can be a useful way of beginning to deal with a seemingly insoluble problem.

The two main **principles** of brainstorming are:

deferment of judgement and *quantity breeds quality*

Brainstorming is only a process to begin a discussion – a way of collecting ideas. Time must be allowed afterwards for clarification and discussion, particularly when sensitive issues are raised.

How to brainstorm

1   Make sure that everyone can see what is being written. The best method is to use a flipchart or chalkboard.
2   The issue to be brainstormed should be clearly defined. It can be helpful to have the subject of the brainstorm in the form of a title at the top or in the middle of the sheet of flipchart paper.
3   Suggestions should be succinct – words or phrases rather than sentences – but clarification should wait until the end of the session.
4   Ideas should be 'off the top of the head' – the more creative and off-key the better.
5   Points should be called out to the scribe as quickly as possible – the writing speed of the scribe is the only speed limit.
6   The scribe should make no attempt to put the suggestions in any form or order – brainstorming should have a random air about it to encourage creative thinking. Re-shaping and ordering come after the brainstorm.
7   Judgement must be suspended. No comments about the ideas, or requests for amplification, should be made during the brainstorming. No discussion or signs of approval or criticism should be allowed until the brainstorming is exhausted.
8   Speed is important. As soon as it becomes apparent that ideas are drying up, or that the silences are becoming longer, finish the brain-storm.

Bringing new members to the team

The new procedures were more ethically based and they recognized both that effective teams are those in which there is some creative tension, and that members should be appointed to a team through a different definition of merit. It was agreed that people would not be appointed because of who they know, because they simply have a similar background to the rest of the team, or because they would put up least resistance to the running of the team. Rather they would be appointed because they have a professional background and experience which would enrich the team's productivity, and because they could offer qualities which other members lack. The different approach to problem-solving this might bring would probably be because the new team members are not necessarily part of the dominant discourse of education – white, male and middle-class. Indeed, it was after the introduction of these procedures that many inner city schools appointed more women managers, and more leaders from ethnic minorities – important role models for the young people in inner city schools.

There were some problems with the new procedures – it would be impossible to make a precise science out of something so imprecise as human interaction. Some team leaders regretted the loss of reliance on their intuition or hunches. But intuition is socially constructed and culturally biased. Others felt that the rigidity of the process meant the suppression of important evidence, but the best procedures allowed for the disclosure of relevant evidence – and not clandestinely. Certainly they were an improvement on the previous procedures, as the statistics of increased access to power of women and people from ethnic minorities show.

Some of the lessons learnt from these equal opportunities selection procedures are very important ones. Even those people who are not involved in a formal recruitment procedure may find the framework a useful one to employ when thinking about inviting people to join their team. Many of the most thoughtful selection procedures incorporate the following stages to ensure that the most creative team is built up:

- A panel is drawn from people who are both inside and outside the team, who have responsibility for the well-being of the team, and who represent men and women, and people from ethnic minorities, so that all points of view and experiences are represented (and so that the selected interviewees should never feel that they are in a minority of one).
- The process begins with an exit interview, or the equivalent – in other words, a discussion with the out-going team member to ask for their comments about the job they are leaving, and for any suggestions they might have to improve the job in the future.
- The same team of panel members draws up the job description, the personal specification, the long list, the short list and the interview questions, and holds the interview.
- The job description reflects the relevant input from the departing postholder, suggestions from the rest of the team, ideas from members of the panel, and the philosophy of the school and department. In other words, it is not duplicated automatically from the previous incumbent's job description – a scrupulous reassessment is advisable each time.
- The wording of the advertisement, the job description and the person specification, is examined with care for language which

might be in a particularly powerful discourse and which might thus disempower the very people you would like to encourage to apply. For example, words and phrases such as: 'thrusting and dynamic', 'intelligent', 'high-achieving', 'proven record of success', and 'good track record', all make some prospective candidates turn the page quickly to another advertisement! They come from a driven, competitive, sporting background, and they have little to do with empowering and facilitating learning and teaching.

- The advertisement is placed in journals and papers which have a wide circulation, not ones which are only read by and strongly reflect a narrow part of society – the trawl for good people needs to be as wide as possible.
- The criteria for short listing are closely connected with the published job and person specifications. They will be agreed by the panel, and used by *all* the panel, preferably in a meeting, in order to invite a selection of candidates to interview.
- The panel agrees a set of questions to be asked of all the candidates, and to be shared out equally between them so that no-one sits silent at the interview, and no-one dominates it. The chair of the panel has special responsibility here, particularly during the interview itself.
- At the interview, it is made clear that this is a two-way process, where the best candidate is to be selected, but also where the candidates will be put at their ease in order to be encouraged to interview well. In this way, the panel will be able to make a more informed decision about the person they eventually choose.
- After the chosen candidate has accepted the post, the unsuccessful people will be told as soon and as carefully as possible. They will be offered feedback on the interview if they wish to receive it.
- The successful candidate will go through an induction procedure which is designed to be as supportive and enabling as possible. The whole team will be aware that the new member will necessarily make a difference to the way the team functions (see the next but one section 'The life cycle of teams'), and a form of celebration and welcome acknowledges the beginning of a new era for the whole team.

If this procedure is adopted, or if the framework is used to decide which people to invite onto work teams, the team leader will be faced with a group of people who have very different ways of working, and who bring very different qualities to the team. Because of these differences, they may find it difficult to respect each other and to work together constructively. If some of these tensions are understood, it is easier for the team leader to work with their team and to help them to work together.

Key team roles

Useful People to have in Teams

Plant   Advances new ideas and strategies with special attention to major issues and looks for possible breaks in approach to the problems with which the group is confronted. Is creative, imaginative, and unorthodox.

Resource investigator   Explores and reports on ideas, developments and resources outside the group; creates external contacts that may be useful to the team and conducts any subsequent negotiations. Is extrovert, enthusiastic and communicative.

Chair   Controls the way in which a team moves towards the group objectives by making the best use of team resources; recognizes where the team's strengths and weaknesses lie; and ensures that the best use is made of each team member's potential. Is mature and confident, and clarifies goals while promoting decision-making and delegates well.

Shaper   Shapes the way in which team effort is applied; directs attention generally to the setting of objectives and priorities; and seeks to impose some shape or pattern on group discussion and on the outcome of group activities. Is challenging and dynamic, and thrives on pressure while having the drive and confidence to overcome obstacles.

Monitor-evaluator   Analyses problems and evaluates ideas and suggestions so that the team is better placed to take balanced decisions. Is sober, strategic and discerning, and judges situations accurately.

Team worker   Supports members in their strengths (e.g. building on suggestions); underpins members in their shortcomings; improves communications between members and fosters team spirit generally. Is co-operative, mild, perceptive and diplomatic. Listens, builds, averts friction, and calms.

Implementer   Turns concepts and plans into practical working procedures; carries out agreed plans systematically and efficiently. Is disciplined, reliable and conservative.

Completer   Ensures that the team is protected as far as possible from mistakes of both commission and omission; actively searches for aspects of work which need a more than usual degree of attention; and maintains a sense of urgency within the team. Is painstaking, conscientious and anxious.

Specialist   Is single-minded, self-starting and dedicated. Provides knowledge and skills in rare supply.

Source: R. Meredith Belbin (1997 reprint) *Team Roles at Work*, Butterworth Heinemann

Meredith Belbin first published a very interesting piece of research about the most useful people to have in teams, in 1981 (Belbin, 1981). He found that there were some important roles that are essential to the creativity and productivity of a team. In 1993 he revised his original terms in order to refine them more clearly and to take into account some of the more sexist interpretations (Belbin, 1993). He listed the nine sets of personality traits shown on page 21, making it clear that combinations of these characteristics can reside in one person – thus it is not necessary to have nine people in every team – but good teams should include a group of people who between themselves are able to operate in all these ways.

An effective team leader will be particularly aware of these necessary different ways of operating, because they can cause friction. For example, the drive and originality of the shaper can irritate and be irritated by the painstaking orderliness of the completer. Or the sober prudence of the monitor-evaluator may well exasperate the unorthodox and individualistic plant. I have been in teams where someone had exciting original ideas squashed immediately by a pernickety completer who could not live with the messiness of creativity, and I have seen marvellously innovative schemes put into seemingly effortless operation by supportive teamworkers, implementers and completers. Although Heads of Department may not automatically chair meetings, a major part of their responsibility to the team will be to make sure that they all work together.

Clearly the implications of Belbin's work for a Head of Department are that an awareness of these necessary characteristics ensures both that teams are built up around differences, and that the differences are celebrated and welcomed. When a team appears not to function as well as it could, a completion of the Belbin inventory will show what characteristic is missing. The person responsible for the team will then either find someone to fill the gap, or will encourage the team to develop new ways of working together to make up for the missing way of working.

The life cycle of teams

A reflection on all teams that one has worked in will show that they vary in size, that some are permanent and some are very temporary, and that they all have different ways of working. A Head of Department may have responsibility for or be part of a curriculum team, a pastoral team, a middle management team and maybe several different working parties and action groups.

Taking into account the discussion in the previous section about the differences team members bring with them, and that new team members herald the beginning of a new team, it will become apparent that teams are never static in their dynamics. The energy they arouse seems to give them a life cycle of their own. In order to think more clearly about this aspect of the lives of teams, it might be simpler to focus on a class of young people whose emotional impact on middle managers is often more distant and easier to make sense of than that of the other adults to be managed.

The fluidity and development of the relationship between teacher and class may be a helpful example of the dynamics of a team. The thoughts about the changes in the class over a school year can then be transferred to the teams of adults for whom a Head of Department has a management responsibility or with whom they work. The framework I would like to introduce does not necessarily fit every group, class or team closely – some appear to miss out some of the stages in their development. It may also seem a little simplistic. But it is a useful basic theoretical framework on which to base reflections and discussion about the ways teams work, and it might be a helpful way of reflecting on the general activities in a curriculum team, or indeed any team of adults within a school.

All teachers are aware that their relationships with the classes they teach are different, and that the classes are more or less difficult to work with at different times in the academic year. There is a great deal of writing about group development, because this has been an area of research since the 1930s. Just as experienced teachers come to expect changing relationships with classes as the academic year progresses, so sensitive team leaders will be aware of the effects of group dynamics when working with their teams of colleagues. There follows a very simple description of the usual life cycle of teams. Obviously teams move between and amongst the stages described more raggedly than the description initially suggests. More rigorous writing on this subject can be found in the works of Bion (1968), Adair (1986) and Jaques (1991).

Forming. Teams may go through a 'honeymoon' period for a short time very early in their lives as a team. At this point, they behave very formally and politely. They are anxious and ask many questions of the team leader and about the task. They seem to be trying to work out the rules necessary to achieve the task.

Storming. This can be a very uncomfortable time for team leaders *and* team members. This is when conflict and sub-groups emerge, and the authority of the leader is challenged. Opinions polarize and individual team members resist the efforts of the team leader or the group, to gain control. This is an emotional stage where basic values and the achievability of the task are questioned.

Norming. After the storm comes the quiet. The group begins to work together more agreeably, developing mutual support, reconciling some differences and celebrating others. Co-operation begins in order to work on the task, ground rules are agreed on, and communication of views and feelings develop.

Performing. This can be a very satisfying stage. The group organizes itself into a team in order to form an appropriate structure for the task to be completed. There is a general air of progress as team members move flexibly between group roles. There is a positive energetic ethos to the team at this stage.

Some teams need to go through a *mourning* stage before they begin to *form*. This means that they constantly refer back to their previous teams, and show signs of sadness and an inability to accept the need for a new team. They may say things such as 'We liked it better the other way', or 'Why do we always have to change things?'

Many schools, because of their academic year, are constantly forming groups which then have to *adjourn*. The nature of schools demands that pupils and teachers end groups and teams as soon as they reach the *performing* stage because the task is done or because the year is over.

An understanding of these stages can make it easier for a team leader to stay hopeful about the team even when it is at some of the uncomfortable stages in the lives of teams. For example, it might be helpful to remember:

- Even one new member of a team can change the dynamics so that the team feels as though it is a new team, and that it is embarking on the whole life cycle again.
- If the team leader imports a new team member in order to make the team more effective, re-forming the team and going through some of the more uncomfortable stages can have very positive outcomes.
- The storming stage can be almost imperceptible (especially if the team is made up of very sophisticated communicators), or it can be very upsetting and full of conflict.
- The aftermath of the storming stage is a very productive stage, and usually a team must go through the storming stage before it becomes effective.
- It is important that the team leader attempts to lead the team through the storming stage so that it does not stay in that stage unproductively and painfully for too long.
- If a team seems to be caught in the storming stage, it could be very beneficial to the team to talk about the stages of team life – to look carefully together at the conflict and storming.
- The adjourning stage is easier to cope with if it is acknowledged. Schools are not very good at endings – they usually occur before we are ready for them. An effective team leader can plan ahead for ending celebrations which suitably acknowledge the achievements of the team.

Although some people are discouraged from working with teams because of the energy consumed by the dynamic interactions, this section is written partly as an explanation of those interactions, and partly as an encouragement to become involved in teamwork. It may seem that teams can be emotionally 'messy' organizations in which people struggle to make order and preserve autonomy. But the energy and creativity liberated when a team has gone through its storming and norming stages and entered the performing stage can be harnessed to produce marvellous work. At the performing stage, it is very exciting and confirming to be a team member, and well worth some of the previous discomfort.

Working with people

Space has been spent so far praising the work which teams can do together, and encouraging Heads of Department to develop teams in spite of some of the acknowledged difficulties. But it is very important not to lose sight of the individuals inside the teams, and of the task to be completed by the team. John Adair (1986) introduces a very simple diagram (see Figure 2.1) to remind managers to balance individual needs with team needs and the needs of the task.

He reminds team leaders that it is important to keep all three sets of needs in balance. In other words, when a team seems overpowered or paralysed by the needs of one person, it is important that the person who has responsibility for the well-being of the team takes time to reflect on the problem. First it is important to try to understand the individual's need, then it is necessary to see how the individual's needs balance with the needs of the whole team, and with the necessity to complete the task.

Take, for example, a team meeting. Perhaps there is suddenly an urgent need to meet as a department because the Senior Management Team is asking for new and vital planning information which will affect the following year's pupil:teacher ratio in the school. You must meet as a team to discuss

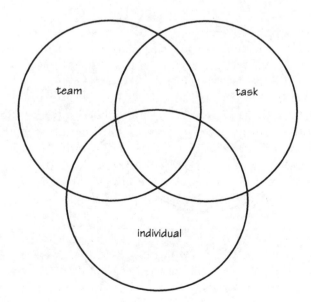

Figure 2.1   Balancing needs

timetable allocations for next year, as soon as possible. So the immediacy of the task is clear.

It is also clear that the outcomes of this planning exercise will have a direct and far-reaching effect on the workloads of members of your department – there is little argument about the need to meet as a team as soon as possible. And you all agree that you can find an hour to meet before school the next morning – some people are willing to make long journeys even earlier than usual because they recognize the importance of the meeting.

However, one member of the team cannot make the meeting – your deputy Head of Department. His child will be starting school for the first time in the morning – the first day at school. And it has long been arranged that he will be an hour or two late into school, so that he can help his child to settle in. Here we have an irrefutably important individual need, of an important team member. If this set of needs is transposed on to Adair's diagram it appears as shown in Figure 2.2.

Of course, this problem is underpinned by the ethical premise that every-one on a team should have a voice (the second principle at the beginning of the section 'Working with teams'). It may even be irrelevant that the team member who cannot attend the meeting is the Deputy Head of Department. If you believe that everyone should have a say, you will be committed to encouraging *everyone* to attend and to speak and be listened to.

The starkest alternatives are to cancel the meeting and write the bid yourself; to carry on with the arranged meeting without the input of the team member; or to ignore the immediacy of the demand from the Senior Management Team and to decide to get in a bid from your department when

the team
must meet
as soon as
possible

allocating
the
teaching
loads

an important team
member has a very
valid reason for
absence

Figure 2.2   Balancing needs in practice

you are ready. This last alternative would probably mean missing the deadline. So each of these solutions fails completely to answer one of the needs to be balanced – the achievement of the task.

Cancelling the meeting altogether would mean that the needs of an individual member were overpowering the needs of the team *and* stopping the task being achieved. Holding the meeting without the input of the team member would be a punitive action, and would ensure that the team met without its full problem-solving capacity. To go back to the diagram, the object is to maintain a balance so that all three needs are represented and no one of the three needs dominates the other two.

In order to keep the balance, compromise is necessary – would the SMT be happy to postpone the date for the reception of the information? Could a working party of representatives from the team meet in order to make the plans? Would it be possible to ask the Deputy Head of Department for his suggestions, and to feed them into the meeting, so that his voice would be heard although he could not attend in person?

When a seemingly insurmountable problem arises in the management of your team, and when you feel yourself to be convinced by one need to the detriment of the others in the equation, Adair's balance might be a way of finding time for reflection and reaching an equitable conclusion.

Another imbalance might arise when members of your team have a constellation of personal problems which are stopping them from working well. Education is about developing people, management is about understanding and developing people – a Head of Department cannot ignore the pain and difficulty of a struggling department member. It may be that all your counselling skills are called on, and it may become necessary for you to spend a great deal of your time with this particular team member. A good team has time and space for short periods of individual malfunction. It is probably usually possible for an organization like a school to allow one set of needs to dominate for a short while, but in general the three constituents only work productively when in balance. Thus it is important to keep a mental picture of the balance of needs – is the team still able to function? Is the team still achieving the necessary tasks?

If the difficulties stop the team from functioning for long periods, it might be necessary to suggest to the relevant team members that they go for professional counselling, or maybe for medical attention. The fine balance is between being taken over completely by seemingly insoluble problems and allowing those problems to overcome a whole team, and ignoring the needs of one team member to such an extent that they are excluded from the team.

Listening to and talking to department members

A Head of Department will come to more constructive solutions to problems with colleagues if time can be found to think carefully, and if it is possible to be reminded of educational values and a philosophy of management. Unfortunately, these more measured responses take time, and a Head of Department is often even more short of time, and has even more competing demands on what little time there is. All the best writing about managing time suggests that activities are prioritized, and careful plans made of the order in which activities are to be carried out. It is necessary to keep to the timing planned for each activity. If colleagues define themselves primarily as teachers, they will plan their timing all around the activities connected with the learning and teaching in which they are primarily involved. But it is the responsibility of a Head of Department to help other teachers with *their* learning and teaching. And here there can be conflict and irritation for people who have not clarified priorities for themselves.

A short scenario

A recognizable scenario might be that you are about to take a class with a particularly challenging group of young people. You have planned a lesson which you know will work as long as the scheme which you have prepared, and which includes rearranging the classroom, is in place before the class arrives. You are hurrying along the corridor, laden with equipment, when an anxious member of your department stops you and insists that you deal with their problem, immediately.

If you are human, your instant reaction will be of intense frustration and irritation at potentially having your teaching plans thwarted. The temptation will be to sweep your colleague out of the way, flattening them with a frustrated and irritated retort. It may well be that you know the problem well already, and that you think it has lower priority than several other departmental problems with which you are grappling at the same time, and than the teaching in which you are so involved at that moment.

But, your responsibility to manage a department includes working constructively with the other teachers in the department. A thoughtful Head of Department will probably have decided that working with colleagues is as important as working with young people. Dealing with the 'interruption' in the corridor on your way to your teaching is as much your responsibility as your teaching. Perhaps it would be clearer if you do not see it as an interruption, but as another facet of your job. And all your interpersonal skills will be necessary in order to balance all your responsibilities particularly in as stressful a situation as this.

A solution to the problem?

Let us go back into the corridor, to the distressed colleague. As a manager, you learn quickly that everyone you work with has their own set of priorities. Everyone sees life differently, and one person's most distressing occurrence may have little significance for another person. But membership of a team demands input from everyone. So the shared significance is that there *is* distress and this distress is blocking the activity of the department or a member of it. It must be dealt with understandingly – dealing with someone else's distress by minimizing or ignoring it compounds the distress. The most important part of working with somebody else's pain is often the acknowledgement of it – you do not have to share it. And as long as your colleague knows that you understand the power of the distress, and knows that you *will* listen and try to help, it is usually not necessary to do so immediately. So the scene in the corridor might read like this:

> [*Head of Department bustles down a corridor laden with equipment, trailing an electric lead, anxious to reach a classroom ten minutes before the end of break in order to set up the classroom. An Anxious Colleague rushes after the Head of Department, attempting to grab a sleeve to get attention*]
>
> *Head of Department:* Oh! Hello, I didn't realize it was you. Are you OK?
>
> *Anxious Colleague:* No, I'm not! You've really got to do something about . . . .
>
> *Head of Department:* Sorry to interrupt – this sounds as if I really need to listen carefully. I'm in a hurry at the moment, so I can't do you justice. Can it wait for a while? We obviously need more time than I have now. Can we agree a time to meet in my room?
>
> *Anxious Colleague:* Yes, of course – what about after school today?
>
> *Head of Department:* I've got a meeting then, but I can talk to you during morning break tomorrow – why don't we have coffee together in my room then?
>
> *Anxious Colleague:* Fine, thanks – it'll wait till then.
>
> [*They each go off in opposite directions to carry on with the rest of their teaching*]

What has happened here has taken less than one minute, but has been satisfactory for both people. The anxious colleague knows that a problem has been acknowledged, and that an agreed time and space has been set aside to talk about it properly. The Head of Department, with a very minor interruption, can carry on with the activity planned for the moment. However, a problem has been acknowledged, and a suggestion has been made that fits in with both their timetables. Agreeing a mutually convenient time allows for both people's full attention, so that the eventual discussion will feel less like an unwelcome interruption.

Often, a colleague's distress is difficult to understand because we do not find the same circumstances distressing. In a busy working life, it is difficult to be sympathetic to someone with whom you do not share particular feelings of distress. On the other hand, a colleague's distress may start off a chain reaction of distress for you: for example, less experienced teachers might wish to work through some of their teaching difficulties with you, and the recounting of difficult classroom dynamics could stir painful memories about your own disturbing early classroom experiences. Lack of sympathy or the arousal of painful memories both make good listening difficult, especially when you do not seem to have enough time for activities with which you feel more at ease. If you find yourself reacting adversely to requests for this type of help, stop, and go back to your underpinning philosophy of management.

Managing a department is about enabling the other teachers in the department to deliver the learning and teaching all have agreed on. When colleagues are struggling with the delivery of the agreed teaching, good listening is required from the Head of Department in order to help colleagues deal with the distress that is stopping them work productively. Good listening includes:

- paying attention to an appropriate atmosphere
- an awareness of non-verbal communication
- care with verbal communication
- an understanding of the barriers to good listening

all of which are underpinned by an understanding of the balance of power between the listener and the one who is being listened to.

Moving on to the following day of the scenario between the Head of Department and the Anxious Colleague, it is possible see how good listening and an awareness of the power balance between the two shape the interview.

An appropriate atmosphere

They have already gone some way to arranging an appropriate atmosphere by choosing a mutually convenient time when each person can give attention to the problem. The cup of coffee and the quiet room also help. Closing the door and taking the phone off the hook will ensure privacy and minimize distraction, but they will also give a message to the distressed colleague that they are important enough to warrant full attention. In a school where there is insufficient quiet space for such interviews, it may be appropriate to arrange a set of signals which create privacy for those who share space.

Wherever possible, it is important to sit where each person can be seen easily, for example, at right angles to each other on chairs of similar height – physical barriers like desks and chairs of different heights reinforce feelings of distance, vulnerability and lack of equality on the part of the person who is in the lower chair and who does not have a desk to lean on or hide behind.

An awareness of non-verbal communication

These points may seem very simplistic, but it is easy to allow attention to wander. Listeners hope that it has not been noticed, and often it has not been, quite consciously. Unconsciously, however, messages of boredom and inattention are given, both of which compound a sense of lack of importance or powerlessness. So it is absolutely necessary to think about eye-contact (a culturally complicated issue, but an important one); about non-verbal prompts such as nodding, silences, and facial expressions; and about whether the way the listener is sitting signifies interest, attention or boredom.

Care with verbal communication

It is important to listen, and not to be tempted to tell people what you think they are going to say. So the Head of Department will not begin the conversation by saying:

'I know exactly how you feel'

or

'So and so told me that you wanted to tell me about . . .'

or

'I hear that . . . .'

Even when the story has been heard from elsewhere, it is always different from each protagonist. By telling the 'opposition's' story, the listener accepts it as truthful, and thus arouses many of the uncomfortable feelings calmed by making this distanced appointment. This meeting is probably as much about distressful and difficult feelings as much as passing information. In fact, the most helpful invitation to begin the story might be as a simple as 'How is it going?' or 'Tell me . . . .'

Listening well does not mean sitting in silence, trying to remember all that is said; nor does it mean constant interruptions to explain that the same thing happened to the listener! The first example is uncanny, and speakers often think that they are not being heard. In the second way of acting, speakers are sure that they are not being heard.

The balanced and empowering listener encourages the speaker to set the agenda, then gently helps, with careful questions, to focus on the real problem:

'Do you mean . . .?'

'Why do you think that was happening?'

Some prompts encourage more talking, but silences should be allowed: when someone is distressed, it is sometimes difficult to talk coherently or in complete sentences. It is helpful to make it clear that hesitation is acceptable and this may be achieved by using encouraging sounds such as 'Ummm', 'Ye – e -s', 'Go on', 'I see', or just by waiting.

If the listener has not understood, if they did not hear properly, or if there are inconsistencies in the story, it is absolutely acceptable to clarify points. But gently and with humility. Clarifying questions such as:

'You mean . . . .'

'I didn't understand, could you tell me that again?'

'Can you give me an example?'

all show that careful listening is taking place and that the listener is keen to understand what is happening.

Understanding the barriers to good listening

The Head of Department has shown an understanding of the barriers to good listening by choosing a time when there are no competing demands on time and attention. The problem is, however, that life in schools is so fast and so all-consuming that when teachers stop physically, their minds often race on. So, it is difficult to slow their thinking down enough to listen well. The temptation is to finish sentences for those who are struggling to articulate difficult feelings, to make action lists or shopping lists, to listen to half sentences and finish them completely differently in their minds from the way that the speaker intended, to water parched plants, or to tidy the desk.

Another problem is that the listener might have such a well-developed set of values about education that those they are listening to are judged against them all the time. It is hard to listen well when the listener has to hear that someone has acted in a way with which they passionately disagree.

Good listening takes practice, and all teachers could well use some practice. Suggested Activity 10 may help here.

Suggested Activity 10

Another entertaining exercise to use at the beginning of a staff development day or a departmental meeting is one that we use as an introductory exercise to our courses.

In pairs, spend *five minutes each*, telling each other what the rest of the group does not know about them, and what they may want the group to hear about:
- their professional journey towards their present professional position
- what they might be doing in two years' time
- some expectations of this meeting
- some ability or skill they have that no-one in the department knows about.

No note-taking!

Each person then reports back to the small group about their 'partner', spending not more than *one minute.*
Then *take two minutes* back in pairs to check that the reports were substantially acceptable.

After the completion of this activity, the team will not only have learnt something new about each other, but they will be able to discuss 'good listening' based on the exercise they just did together. Banning note-taking means that they will have to concentrate on understanding important points immediately, then on remembering them.

Giving and receiving constructive feedback

Heads of Department sometimes feel very vulnerable because they think that their professional activities are so transparent and that everything they do is open to criticism. It is more positive to think about constructive feedback rather than 'criticism'. The emphasis is therefore put on a positive and constructive activity instead of a negative and destructive one. It is also important to remember that a Head of Department must be as ready to receive feedback as to give it – the two-way process models the developmental nature of a helpful interaction. Feedback on the work of an individual (for example, after classroom observation), or how a group is interacting and working together, can offer a different perspective to the listener and others, and the effect their behaviour may have on others.

Constructive feedback is informative, allowing the listener to become more aware of how they behave. It develops communication skills. Constructive feedback is not always *positive feedback; negative feedback* can be very useful, but must be given skilfully so that the recipient does not feel undermined. *Destructive feedback* leaves the recipient demoralized, angry or ashamed, with nothing positive to build on.

Giving feedback

As a manager, a Head of Department is often expected to give those they manage feedback about their work.

1 *Start with the positive.* There is a tendency whenever doing a critical appraisal to look for mistakes and emphasize the negative. It is much more encouraging (and effective) to start with the positive – what was liked and worthy of note. Negative points will be listened to and acted upon more readily if good points have been acknowledged first.

2 *Be specific.* General comments (for example, 'brilliant' or 'awful') are not very helpful. Talk about specific skills and incidents rather than general sweeping impressions.

3 *Refer only to what* **can** *be changed (with negative feedback).* It is not helpful to comment on areas where there is no choice (for example, facial or bodily characteristics). Concentrate on improvements which can be changed or developed (for example, body language).

4 *Offer alternatives.* It is not supportive simply to criticize when offering negative feedback – offer alternatives (for example, if someone in a group discussion has been ignored, suggest ways in which she/he could have been brought in).

5 *Be descriptive rather than evaluative.* Don't make value judgements. Say just what you saw and heard and the effect this had on you. Make clear that you are giving *your own views.* So use 'I saw . . .', or 'I heard . . .' and 'In my opinion . . .', to start sentences, rather than 'You are . . .' or 'You did . . .'.

6 *Leave the other person with a choice.* Do not try to impose your own views. This can lead to resistance and disbelief. Skilled feedback gives people information about themselves in a way which offers them choices – including the option *not* to change.

7   *Consider what the feedback says about you.* Feedback – what you choose to comment on, and how you say it – will say as much about you as about the receiver. It will reveal your own values and behaviour. You can learn something about yourself if you think about the feedback you are giving – and *how* you are giving it.

Receiving feedback

Managers expect to receive feedback on their work from those they manage as well as those who manage them. They can learn a lot and develop their skills by asking for feedback. They encourage the giver by using some of the above skills but they will also benefit by the following.

1   *Listening to the feedback rather than immediately rejecting or arguing about it.* Feedback may sometimes make the recipient feel uncomfortable but it is healthier to encourage and learn from it than immediately to bristle and deny. The listener can learn a great deal about themselves by trying to assess comments objectively. At a very basic level, people will have views about you and it is better that you are aware of them than that they hide them for fear of incurring your wrath. But you are also entitled to your view and to ignore any comment which you think irrelevant, inaccurate, given for the wrong reason or given by someone whose judgement you do not trust.

2   *Be clear about what is being said.* Make sure you understand what is *really* being said before you respond to feedback. Don't jump to conclusions or become defensive. Always check back if the meaning is not clear.

3   *Check with others rather than relying on one source.* People have different perceptions of the behaviour of others. Check with others that the opinion is a shared one. This will often give you a more balanced view of your actions.

4   *Ask for feedback you want but don't get.* Feedback is important in many situations. Do not be shy of asking for feedback if it has not been offered when you feel it will help you.

5   *Decide what you will do as a result of the feedback.* You should use feedback to develop your own skills. You should assess its value, and the consequences of ignoring or using it, and then make a positive decision about action or inaction.

Feedback is not easy, but it is a valuable practice in any organization or relationship. Always acknowledge the value of the process to the person who has provided you with feedback.

Recording information

The next problem that a busy Head of Department in this position may face is that of retaining information. However good the formal information systems of a school are, informal messages and information passed in the corridor, hurriedly and elliptically, are more difficult to manage.

Reflecting back on the scene in the corridor, it becomes clear that a diary is an indispensable and constant necessity. Carrying round a well-organized diary which has a user-friendly shape and size means that many discussions can be halved – it is not necessary to get back to people if a decision can be made immediately about when people are free, and if it can be noted at the moment the arrangement is made. The minds of busy Heads of Department are rather like an overworked computer – they sometimes 'junk' important information because it has not been stored properly. It would be helpful if the well-organized diary also had spaces for lists and for notes. It is also useful to attach both a pen and pencil to the diary permanently, and to make appointments initially in pencil – busy organizations constantly reorganize timings and meetings, and nothing is more discouraging to someone who is struggling to keep a readable diary than to have to remove or change appointments that are written in ink.

Other types of notes – those private and judgemental ones made or received about colleagues and young people – are more problematic, and probably rightly so. I was a Pastoral Head in a secondary school when it became clear that the law had changed to allow people right of access to their files. The parents of young people and beyond a certain age, the young people themselves, have access (with certain exemptions) to any records kept about them. Initially, the staff were annoyed because it meant that we had to go back over many files to make sure that they were clearly written and had no libellous material in them. But I am glad that we did so. Sometimes I was shocked at the thoughtless, judgemental, passionate notes some of us had written to each other about young people. I was also struck by how the behaviour and activities described had changed since we began recording them – the activity was described crudely, and recording it meant that it was preserved as if in aspic – but the young person had often developed more positively than we had expected, and left that behaviour behind.

The guides to the law for school governors of county, controlled and special agreement schools, grant maintained schools, aided schools and special schools state the following. (This is taken from the guide to the law for school governors of county, controlled and special agreement schools, but it is written almost identically in the guides for governors of all the above schools.)

Pupils' Educational Records

12 Governing bodies are required to keep a curricular record of each pupil – a formal record of academic achievements, other skills and abilities, and progress in school. They must update this every year. Other material may be recorded on this record, such as details of behaviour and family background, but this is not compulsory. This material, without the notes that a teacher makes for his or her use only, makes up the pupil's educational record.

13 Within 15 school days of being asked, governing bodies must allow the following people access to records, apart from the material listed in paragraph 16 below:

• a parent of the pupil (for pupils under 16);

- parents and pupils (for pupils aged 16 and 17);
- the pupil only (for pupils aged 18 or over);
- the head of any independent school, or the governing body of any other school, or the head of a further or higher educational establishment which the pupil has applied to.

(p. 70)

16 Certain information held in a pupil's record may not be disclosed. The Education (School Records) Regulations 1989 explain which information in detail, but briefly they prevent disclosure of:
- material supplied by anyone other than employees of the LEA or Educational Welfare Officers;
- material whose disclosure might cause serious harm to the pupil or someone else;
- material concerning actual or suspected child abuse;
- material concerning other pupils;
- references supplied to potential employers of the pupil, and national body concerned with student admissions, another school, an institution of further or higher education, or any other place of education or training;
- reports by a school to a juvenile court; or
- ethnically based data.

(p. 71)

(*School Governors – a Guide to the Law – County, Controlled and Special Agreement Schools*, DfEE, 1994)

The Data Protection Act 1984 is about access to and privacy for information kept on computers. Most schools have probably chosen to register under the terms of the Act. More information about it can be found in the DFE's letter of November 1991 'Data Protection Act 1984: Implications for LEA maintained/aided/special schools.'

This Act is an example of a felicitous law which changed, widened and enriched practice. We had to learn to be much more objective and circumspect in our descriptions of interactions with young people – now we might describe it as more professional. The required reflection made us think much more creatively and positively about the actual interactions, and helped change our attitudes and behaviour. It certainly made us think more clearly about the rights of the young people, not only to see their records, but more fundamentally to be described in positive and helpful terms, rather than dismissive and restrictive terms. We were forced to accept them more as partners in the learning and teaching, and less as creatures to whom knowledge was to be transmitted. And we began to think about the power to give or withhold information that we could exercise over the young people with whom we worked.

Delegating

It may seem that writing about delegation at this point is an irrelevance. Many people are tempted to connect delegation with time management, and to see it as a way of making more time by getting rid of unnecessary or unappealing tasks. It is a far more constructive activity than that, and is closely allied to staff development. Far from saving time, it initially takes more time in order to delegate effectively, but eventually, the team will work better, the delegator and delegatee will have shared important tasks, and the Head of Department will be closely involved in developing new skills in team members. Suggested Activity 11 will help to clarify the importance of delegation in developing teams and teamwork.

Suggested Activity 11

If you complete the following activity with members of your team you will ultimately agree a process which will enrich many of your team interactions.

1   Begin by listing privately all the activities for which you have pro-fessional responsibility.
2   Then put a mark by those you could delegate, if you had suitable people with whom you worked.
3   Then in groups of three or four, discuss points 4 to 7 and attempt to agree on your answers:

4 **Define in one sentence:**

(a) Instruction	(b) Delegation	(c) Abdication

5 **What are the positive and negative factors in delegation (list up to three)?**

(a) For delegators	(b) For the delegatees
Positive:	
Negative:	

---

6 How should you delegate?

(a) Before delegating:	(b) When delegating:
(c) During the task:	(d) After the task:

7 What should or should not be delegated (in normal circumstances)?

Should:	Should not:

8 Now look back at the list you drew up initially. Have you changed your mind about the activities you can delegate?

(Developed by a group of senior school staff on a course run by Beryl Husain)

After thinking about the questions raised in the above activity, it may be that the following points about the process of ethical delegation are raised:

- Beliefs about teambuilding and working with people will inform the planning about delegating: if the aim is to develop and support colleagues into acquiring the expertise to perform tasks they could not perform previously, the process of productive delegation is a most useful framework.
- In order to delegate productively, it is necessary to negotiate carefully with the people to whom the delegator wishes to delegate. Delegation is neither dumping horrible tasks on subordinates, nor briskly telling someone what to do. It requires the use of careful listening skills with which the delegator ensures that the delegator and the delegatee really understand each other, so that misunderstandings can be dealt with, and so that an agreement is reached about the process which both can sustain until the task is completed.
- Effective delegation is *not* principally a way of saving time; at least, not initially. In order to delegate fairly, sufficient time needs to be devoted to the initial discussions so as to make sure that

everyone concerned has agreed both the content of the delegation and the process of the delegation. The transaction may well
fail unless it is carefully agreed, planned and monitored.

- It may be that the delegated tasks are ones that the delegator
could have done faster and more successfully. And some of the
tasks left with the Head of Department may be ones which are
boring and mundane. Delegating is not about getting rid of jobs
people dislike doing. In selecting the tasks to be delegated, it is
helpful to be reminded of underlying principles about management: eventually, the support and encouragement of the team
will entail less work, because other team members are supporting
the team as well.

- It is important to examine decisions about which tasks can be
delegated. Issues of power and habit encourage us to cling to
some tasks which are developmental for other people, and of
which a handover could eventually ease a manager's load. For
example, and I will come back to this in more detail later in this
chapter, chairing meetings. Is it customary for the Head of
Department to chair all departmental meetings? Is it the custom
for the most senior or powerful staff member to chair relevant
meetings? Is this necessary? Here is an example where custom
often dictates unnecessary practice. And careful delegation of
the chairing role could ease the load of the teamleader while
developing important skills in the rest of the team.

Motivation

We do not often think consciously about what motivates us and other people.
Theories of motivation, however, are the framework on which most teaching
and lesson planning is unconsciously built.

Teachers and managers spend a great deal of time trying to understand
why the people they work with do what they do. The main problem is that a
real understanding of what motivates people is difficult because it demands
objectivity, whereas people's behaviour is usually interpreted by the effect it
has on others. Irritation, pleasure or despair are first felt about a colleague's
action, and then if a manager is feeling 'grown up', they try to understand
what in their colleague's action makes them feel like that and why they are
doing what they are doing. If they are not feeling 'grown up', they stay with
their feelings of discomfort or pleasure, and respond only to that effect on
them. Those who receive the feelings are still an important part of the
equation, because they are relying on their own feelings to understand their
colleague's feelings and actions. This is not always appropriate because their
understandings and motivations are constructed by their own backgrounds
and experiences.

Here is a concrete example to illustrate this point:

Your departmental procedures involve a weekly meeting after school, every Thursday, for one hour. There are eight of you, and you each take turns to chair the meetings. One member of your team always arrives late and always leaves early. He sits through the meeting saying nothing unless addressed directly – people comment on his behaviour behind his back because everyone else is so involved in the team's interactions. He is, however, a superb teacher who knows the subject very well. Because he is so unpunctual, he has managed to avoid (the team's interpretation of his motivation for unpunctuality) taking the chair, ever. Indeed, not making him chair, not welcoming him or recapping on the previous decisions of the meeting, and not asking for his opinion when considering team action are all used as forms of punishment for his apparent lack of commitment.

It is easy to interpret other people's silence as disapproval, anger, or lack of commitment, especially if you do not talk together to check out the reality behind that silence. Many people who are not silent see others' silence as powerful, and fill it with their own inadequacy or disapproval of their inadequacy. And these strong negative feelings stop us finding out if our interpretations are correct because if we do we are afraid that they will be confirmed. In other words, many team leaders would find it very difficult to have a simple conversation with the team member in the above example, because they think his lack of commitment is a form of disapproval of their leadership style, and that a conversation with him would confirm this.

Speculation on the reasons for his lack of commitment, putting the greatest fears first, might be:

- He has very strong ideas about how to run a department, and your ways of doing so do not meet with his approval.
- He is just marking time until his retirement or until he gets another job, expending as little energy as possible until he can get his pension or move on.
- He thinks that the National Curriculum, and the Local Management of Schools are attempts to control the activities of teachers and to stifle their professionalism. He sees any activities entered into by teachers in response to political demands as a betrayal of his philosophy of education – his refusal to become involved is a political activity.

But, other reasons might be:

- He is supporting some members of his tutor group through a particularly gruelling time, and he talks to them and listens to them at the end of each day. He then finds it hard to switch his attention to the departmental meeting – he is processing their discussions while ostensibly attending your meeting.

- Part of his success and skill with the young people with whom he works is that he has vivid memories of his own life at that age. He did not enjoy his own schooling because he often felt powerless and incompetent. He determined that he would become a teacher to try and redress that balance for young people like him. But the legacy of his own educational experiences is that he is still reluctant to speak in a group of his peers, or with people whom he perceives as more competent and successful than himself. His silence is that of fear and an inability to enter the discussion.
- He is afraid that you (or the school) will see his home situation as unorthodox, so he has not told you about it in case he is judged as unfit to work with young people. Maybe he has responsibility for the care of a chronically sick parent or partner, or he has sole responsibility for several children. Whatever his personal arrangements, he feels he cannot share them with you, but he must always be out of school by a certain time in order to carry out his *other* obligations.

This may be an extreme case of misunderstanding and lack of communication, but there are nuances here that are easily and commonly recognized. The most important lesson to be learnt is that it is important to talk to team members. Team leaders should remember to check out motivations, without projecting their own onto other people. In our courses, we often ask people to make a list of their motivations in teaching and managing. Their points include wonderful positions on the moral high ground, such as changing the world, helping people to develop to their full potential and so on. When we ask them what they think motivates the people with whom they work, they have a completely different, and often very practical, list which might include money, holidays (and formerly job security). Then we remind them that all managers began as neophyte teachers, and that even the most moralistic teachers have some reality and basic needs in their make-up. Suggested Activity 12 will help explore ideas about motivation further.

Each of the 12 points in this activity is a simple and perhaps obvious suggestion for guidelines for managing with people. But they are the strategies that are easily forgotten when under pressure. And it is sometimes difficult to think about ways of motivating people who have made us feel angry or uncomfortable.

Working with conflict: some general points

This aspect of managing with people is the one which most dissuades teachers from becoming managers. Many people are afraid of conflict, and will go to any lengths to avoid causing it or dealing with it among their colleagues. This fear often stops us from talking simply and calmly to people, and so small issues grow larger as they are avoided and embroidered, instead

Suggested Activity 12

Here is an activity that you might try for yourself, in order to think about motivation within your team. Rate the extent to which you carry out the following approaches in motivating your team.

The scoring is:

5 = yes, 4 = to a great extent,
3 = to some extent,
2 = very little, 1 = no

Score

1 Have you agreed with all your team their main targets and responsibilities, so that you can all recognize achievement? ☐

2 Do you recognize the contribution of each member of the group and encourage other team members to do the same? ☐

3 In the event of success, do you acknowledge and build on it? ☐

4 In the event of setbacks, do you identify what did go well and give constructive guidance for improving future performance? ☐

5 Do you delegate enough? Do you give adequate discretion over decisions and accountability to sub-groups or individuals? ☐

6 Do you show those who work with you that you trust them? ☐

7 Do you hedge them around with unnecessary controls? ☐

8 Does your team have adequate opportunity for professional development? ☐

9 Do you encourage all members of the team to develop their capacities to the full? ☐

10 Is the overall performance of each member regularly reviewed in face-to-face discussion? ☐

11 Do you make sufficient time to talk and listen, so that you understand the unique (and changing) profile of needs and wants in each person, so that you are able to work comfortably with them? ☐

12 Do you positively encourage able people to seek promotion either within or outside their present institution? ☐

of being dealt with immediately. And yet, all good teachers are experts in dealing with conflict with and among young people in the classroom. They are highly skilled at defusing, working with, confronting, or using conflict with and between young people, and often do so automatically. A sureness about working with conflict in the classroom is one of the clear signs of an experienced and effective teacher.

It may well be a pity that we think that conflict must be avoided at all times, and that we see it as damaging. Conflict is at the heart of good drama; if we look back at the stages in the life cycle of teams, the storming stage leads into the most productive stage; and conflict can produce creativity. It is not conflict itself that we should be afraid of, but badly managed and uncontrolled conflict. Suggested Activity 13 may help to explore conflict further.

Suggested Activity 13

Here is a way of thinking about conflict, to be done alone or with a group of colleagues. Hopefully it will encourage ways to see some positive aspects of working with conflict if that has not been possible until now.

1 Take a large sheet of paper and put the word CONFLICT in the middle of it.
2 Brainstorm the word, using a black pen, and making sure that this is a real brainstorm – try to make sure that ideas come fast and furiously, and that they really touch feelings about conflict.
3 When the brainstorm finishes, take a blue pen and draw a circle round all the negative comments about conflict.
4 Take a red pen and draw a circle round all the positive aspects of conflict – you may well find that some of the ideas are both negative and positive.

Often, the negative ideas about conflict come out first – this is because they are so powerful and frightening for some people. As the brainstorm continues more positive ideas are brought forward. Thoughts about creativity and about finally clearing away problems will emerge. The next stage is to think about some principles which might underpin how a team works with conflict, and these will probably emerge more clearly after completing Suggested Activity 14, which focuses on working with difficult people.

Working with conflict: 'difficult people'

This section brings together several of the issues explored in the last two sections. The term 'difficult people' is used very loosely. Some people will have absolutely no trouble in choosing a difficult person to think about – when we do Suggested Activity 14 on our courses many people have difficulty deciding which of several difficult people they would like to concentrate on! However, if people are fortunate enough to work in a school where there is open discussion about disagreements and where there really are no serious problems, they might think about a case where they should be counselling a colleague to think about changing their professional practice, or going for promotion.

Suggested Activity 14

Here is a way of exploring ways of working with difficult people. It requires three people, all of whom have agreed to try to trust each other, who have agreed confidentiality, and who understand about good listening and constructive feedback. For the sake of confidentiality, you might wish to do this exercise with people outside your school. You should all be prepared to enter into a role play and to understand what this might entail. We have found that those people who *do* enter into the roles find this exercise very revealing and rewarding – it helps them to understand the dynamics far more clearly than if they just discussed the problem with two good colleagues.

1   By yourself, write about someone inside or outside your school with whom you find it difficult to work. It could be a colleague, a parent, a governor or a member of the support staff. Be prepared to describe a particular interaction, or a very specific problem to explore. *(15 minutes)*

2   Work in groups of three – people with whom you have an understanding about confidentiality, good listening and constructive feedback. One of the group takes *10 minutes* to describe the personality and the situation to be explored – they set the scene.

3   The person offering the description role plays the person described, and one of the other two role plays the person trying to resolve the situation. The third member of the group acts as observer and keeps time. *(10 minutes)*

4   Spend *10 minutes* giving feedback and discussing the role play. The observer leads the feedback, but all three members of the group should take part in the discussion.

5   Repeat the whole exercise three times, so that everyone has experienced all three roles.

Timekeeping is very important – no matter how absorbing the problem is, try to keep to the times given.

Come back together making sure that you are out of role, and talk about what you learnt from doing this.

It is not helpful to prescribe what you might learn from this activity. Nor is it suggested that you go on a 'magical mystery tour' by completing this activity. Each person who does this role play finds out something different but equally important both about themselves and about the people they are looking at. It offers an opportunity to look at the power of the emotional interaction in a safe environment, and then a more measured chance to use three minds to address one problem. Before our participants do this task, they are aware, and perhaps frightened of, the power of the emotional interaction, but they have not realized the value of the measured chance to use three minds. The emotional aspect frightens them before they do it – the three minds looking at it while holding it safe is the beneficial outcome.

If you have the opportunity to do the above role play, do so, and after completing the activity see whether, as a trio, you can draw out some guidelines for use when working with difficult people. This is an ideal opportunity for drawing general points from a particular issue. Those general points will be very useful in your future dealings with difficult people. The list from people on our courses has included:

- Using a strategy like this one to find the opportunity to reflect, in 'safe' company, about the problem.
- Acknowledging the uncomfortable feelings aroused in you by your difficult person; then trying to put them aside to work objectively with the problem.
- Separating the person from the problem – try to focus more on your shared present difficulty, rather than on your shared history of misunderstanding or animosity.
- Taking time – trying not to react immediately, and therefore making sure that you are not in your usual unproductive pattern with this person. Make time to think quietly about your next action, so that it is proactive rather than reactive.
- Developing a network of people whose values you share and who are in the same sort of position as you, so that you can support each other with each person's difficult people.
- Planning your actions carefully – if you do not have the opportunity to discuss your problem, at least rehearse the next conversation for yourself. Traffic jams and showers are ideal places for loud but private monologues!

These are points to be borne in mind when working with conflict in general, not just in relationship to a specific person. Fear of conflict is so powerful for most managers that the fear confuses the real issues, and the conflict becomes encrusted with irrelevancies such as politics and history.

Working with conflict: disciplining members of staff

'Discipline' is one of those words which induces fear and discomfort in would-be managers, and reminds them of their most fervently-held beliefs of equality and empowerment. They interpret discipline as a harsh form of control. It is more helpful as a manager to think rather of 'encouraging professional behaviour', and to think about the rights of the young people in school to equality and empowerment. It is probably more helpful to think about discipline problems with those whom you manage as times when they are not acting professionally. If the main activity of managing is to ensure that the learning and teaching in your curriculum area is as effective as possible, if a team member shows by their actions that they are not committed to the team's agreed team goals then they need to be taken through a series of clear discussions and warnings until your discussions become formal and are eventually handed over to your senior management.

Before things reach these formal stages, it is important to use the clarifying and distancing strategies listed in the previous section to make sense of what is actually happening. It should be possible, if necessary, for you to talk in confidence and without prejudice with a more senior member of staff in order to isolate and specify the precise activities to be dealt with. By isolating the activities, clear strategies can be planned, based initially on an expectation that your team member has the ability to change for the better. Depending on the severity of the problem, it can be handed over entirely to senior management, or you all can work together towards an agreed and rehearsed solution.

Any discussions with the relevant team member should be informed by the suggestions made earlier in this chapter (see section 'Listening to and talking to department members'), and if the interviews become more serious it is advisable to make careful notes about the outcomes of discussions, detailing any agreed action to be taken, with relevant dates. Local Authorities and schools have grievance and disciplinary procedures which have been carefully worked out with teachers' unions. Mike Ironside and Roger Seifert (1995) have written *Industrial Relations in Schools* which looks at disciplinary procedures in schools. Do not begin these formal procedures on your own – they are quite severe, and need the backing of official channels.

However, it is important to think about the principles which underpin effective disciplinary procedures because they can inform the less formal interactions which precede official procedures – they coincide with the principles which underpin good management:

- care is taken to hear all 'sides' so that the person who is accused of misconduct has a fair hearing and is informed of the grounds for complaint;
- relevant management levels are clarified, so that a middle manager is not left coping with issues of gross misconduct;
- remedial strategies are based on the premise that all people have the ability to improve, and that schools are organizations where everybody is encouraged to learn and develop;
- strategies for improvement are best worked out, agreed, noted and reviewed with relevant dates;
- if agreed action is not forthcoming, then the next negotiated stage should automatically take place.

Staff discipline is a very unclear and difficult area, but it is made easier with care, clear thinking and clarity of communication. And it is an area where it is best, if possible, to plan strategies with those who manage you.

Working with conflict: disciplining young people

All schools have different policies about the behaviour and discipline of the young people who attend. Indeed they have different tolerance levels and different attitudes to those who break the rules. All state schools have developed or are in the process of developing behaviour policies, and other attendant policies such as awards policies and homework policies. In most schools, these policies are framed positively, and are based on optimistic expectations that everyone can improve. If the policies have been developed carefully, all members of staff will have had a contribution to their formation and will be committed to making them work. Some policies include flow-charts to show where teachers can go for help if they have difficulties in the classroom. Heads of Departments often play important roles in these plans, usually as the first person to be approached.

It is easy, as an experienced teacher, to see where less experienced teachers either contribute to the escalation of young people's classroom misbehaviour, or else are seen to ignore or accept unacceptable behaviour, and thus are thought to condone it. Experienced teachers reach a stage of working with young people where they draw boundaries in their interaction with them at a level which appears to an outsider to be intuitive. It is part of the skill of middle management to be able to articulate these boundaries to less experienced teachers. The framework I give in the next section 'Professional Development' in which a Head of Department works with a Beginning Teacher to plan for more successful beginnings to lessons is hopefully a helpful example of this.

The ease with which many Heads of Department work with young people makes it more difficult to hold back from working directly with the young people, and more difficult to work with those they manage, in order to help them to learn to do it themselves. It is a terrible temptation to rush off and 'deal with' a supposed miscreant, rather than spend time talking carefully with the appropriate teacher about what happened, and planning tactics so that it will not happen again. Sometimes the discussions show that the teacher and the young person have reached an impasse, and the Head of Department may have to act as a go-between, or to referee a meeting between them.

Many discussions with teachers about the problems presented by young people begin with the use of such words as 'naughty', 'lazy' or 'difficult'. But in fact, careful discussions often reveal that the behaviour presented by the young person is often a result of deficiencies in curriculum planning and delivery. Has the particular young person access to the teaching and learning on offer? Is the content relevant? Has real differentiation been taken into account? These are questions which an experienced teacher within the same discipline can ask a less experienced teacher. It is part of the role of the Head of Department to explore such issues with members of the department.

In the last few pages, there are some very different examples of the way conflict infuses the daily work of a Head of Department. Suggestions for working with all the examples are based on the need for calm and thoughtful planning, and for the careful disentanglement of powerful feelings from actual activity. It is hoped that plans will be linked to both a philosophy of education and a philosophy of management, which have as a core belief that everyone is driven by finer feelings which include a hopefulness about people, that everyone wishes the best for other people, and that everybody has the potential to develop further.

Professional development

Schools and their staff now have different expectations about professional development, or staff development, from those they had in previous decades. It is one of the aspects of the lives of teachers which has changed most since the middle 1980s. Before then, professional development was mainly thought of as going on courses – it was seen as a private enterprise which had everything to do with the perceived needs of the individual teacher, and little to do with the needs of the department or the school. When I was a school teacher, some teachers I worked with were proud to say that they had never been on a course, while others snatched the *The Times Educational Supplement* as soon as it arrived in order to find a course they might enjoy more than teaching their classes. Both of these attitudes were connected with the belief that being in front of a class was the most important thing that a teacher could do – anything else was escape and of far less value to the teaching and learning in the school.

Another fundamental change is that for state schools the cost of professional development was borne almost entirely by Local Education Authorities until the 1988 Education Reform Act. As a result of that Act, many costs including the costs of professional development were delegated to schools. Most schools have now generated a staff development plan to fit into their school development plan. This is an area in which schools have benefited as a result of the Education Reform Act. Financial responsibility for professional development has raised its profile, and made sure not only that development fits better into school plans, but also that the providers of professional development give value for money. Many teachers find it more difficult to get leave from school to attend courses, and so when they do go, they have higher expectations of the delivery of the course. And when they return to school from this expensive activity, they are expected to report on their learning to their colleagues. Consultants and advisers who are bought in by schools to work with them on the premises must also give good value, and as many of them are former school managers who have been 'rationalized' and then privatized, they have a reputation and a living to keep up.

However, not all professional development is expensive or necessarily offsite: the five compulsory professional development days introduced to schools in 1988 have encouraged the evolution of many different collaborative professional development activities, and schools are far more expert at developing their staff than they used to be.

The next part of this section will examine further the following concepts:

- Does professional development mean only going on courses?
- Is staff development a furtive or individualistic activity?
- Has professional development no connection with school development?
- Is staff development only for the teachers in a school – not for other members of staff?

Some writing and thinking about professional development and adult professional learning is explored and these concepts are addressed.

Theories about professional development

Perhaps the main reason for the narrowness of definition of staff development has been because of misunderstandings of the term INSET. The initials INSET, **IN S**ervice **E**ducation and **T**raining, originally meant just that – education as professional development. But the 'education' part of the description soon got lost, and too often, teachers talked of 'in-service training'. This brought connotations of going away and being *trained*, out of school, often by the Local Authority. The word 'training' seemed to have an air of passivity about it, a lack of active involvement by learners in their learning, and there was often little link between the training offered and the reality of the classroom. Suggested Activity 15 will help to expand the definition of professional development.

Suggested Activity 15

1 Divide your team into two groups, giving each group a sheet of flipchart paper, but making sure that they do not see each other's sheet. In the centre of one sheet, write: INSET. In the centre of the other sheet, write: PROFESSIONAL DEVELOPMENT.

2 Ask each group to brainstorm the words in the centre of their specific flipchart sheet.

3 Compare the flipcharts. It may well be that the group working on INSET has a much narrower set of suggestions than those people working on PROFESSIONAL DEVELOPMENT. However, a comparison of the two should eventually show that 'professional development' includes such ideas as reading books and newspapers, talking, watching television and taking part in effective meetings, which do not need cover and which do not cost money. They can be done on-site, and indeed are part of the expected activities of an exciting school or department.

It is necessary to return to basic beliefs about education and management in order to redefine 'staff development' more fully and creatively. Without doubt, the emphasis is on the word 'development', and maybe the addition of the word 'professional' allows the nature of the activity to be understood more clearly. I have enjoyed reading about professional development in the work of three people: David Kolb (1984), Stephen Brookfield (1993) and Donald A. Schön (1987). Kolb's work is about experiential learning, Brookfield is interested in developing critical thinking, and Schön writes about the reflective practitioner. Their work has been the basis for valuable and insightful writing about professional development by many other teachers. Their particular attraction is that all of them describe the effective learning of professionals as being far away from that transmission model of the student who sits submissively listening to a long, learned and discursive lecture. Rather, in their own ways they describe professional learning as an operation which calls for the active participation of the learner, recognizing that effective learning requires proper acknowledgement of and respect for the learner's experience. The experiences that teachers have in their working lives must be the bases for their learning.

David Kolb (1984) describes his theory about adult experiential learning which makes concrete and practical experience central to the activity of learning. His cycle of learning experience is a very helpful framework on which to base professional development because he works outward from the learner rather than from the teacher. His emphasis is on learning rather than teaching. His cycle need not be followed slavishly and in the order presented below, but this is the basic shape it takes:

1   **concrete experience:** planning for learning must include the opportunity for concrete experience

2   **reflective observation:** reflection on that experience

3   **abstract conceptualization:** an introduction to relevant reading and research findings

4   **active experimentation:** the possibility to plan changes to the concrete, or real, experience next time

5   time to think and talk about that concrete experience

6   and so on.

The stages follow on from each other, and then begin again. Some people see this theory in spiral rather than circular form, so that a developmental aspect is built in.

One important aspect of Kolb's work can be interpreted for professionals who wish to continue to develop their skills and practice – learning does not occur only in meticulously planned courses. Learning occurs everywhere and commonly where practice, reflection, theory, and planning for change are recognized and important. In other words, everywhere where constructive discussion takes place about work.

This cycle will become clearer if Kolb's framework is used to track a common example of professional development in schools. For example, most Heads of Department work with Beginning Teachers, either as part of the latters' teacher education or when they are newly qualified. Some newly qualified teachers seem to know instinctively how to manage one particular aspect of the classroom: how to enter it and how to begin a lesson. Others seem to need endless support and discussion. They often find it difficult to see the problem and to understand it in the first place. Until they do so, they cannot easily make changes in the way they begin their lessons.

Plans to help a Beginning Teacher within a framework based on Kolb's cycle might look like this:

1   **The concrete experience stage:** This could be any one of the first few times the Newly Qualified Teacher or Beginning Teacher (henceforward referred to as NQT) has difficulty beginning a lesson – perhaps this time the young people are there in the room before the lesson begins but they ignore the NQT. It could take ten minutes for the teacher to get their attention, and then only by displaying anger and disapproval, so that an air of discontent pervades the rest of the lesson. It may be that the NQT is aware that the difficulties begin at the start of the lesson, or it maybe that the Head of Department (HOD) has walked past the room and heard the noise. However the conversation between the NQT and the HOD begins, here is a clear and common example of a difficult beginning to a lesson on which to base important professional development.

2   **The reflective observation stage:** This is where significant learning habits are developed and where the HOD's values about education are clearly visible and transmittable. This is the stage where the HOD encourages the NQT to become a reflective practitioner. In order to talk constructively about what often feels like a destructive experience, two issues are important for the HOD:
   – deciding which are the right questions to ask, without apportioning blame or guilt;
   – developing critical thinking with the Beginning Teacher.
   The right question is the one which helps the NQT to think about the problem in such a way as to clarify the issues. It is very difficult to have a constructive discussion about difficult lessons when the conversation is encrusted with guilt and 'should haves'. It is far easier for both parties if more experienced teachers remember their own early efforts at class-

room control, and if they see all difficulties as experiences from which to learn rather than as unforgivable mistakes. The right questions encourage critical thinking.

Stephen Brookfield describes the process of developing critical thinking as that of a *learning conversation.*

> 1   *Good conversations are reciprocal and involving*
> In a good conversation, the participants are continually involved in the process; they are either talking or listening. Developing critical thinking is a process in which listening and contributing are of equal importance.
> 2   *The course of good conversations cannot be anticipated*
> When we begin to ask people to identify assumptions underlying their habitual ways of thinking and learning, we do not know exactly how they are going to respond.
> 3   *Good conversations entail diversity and disagreement*
> A measure of diversity, disagreement, and challenge is central to helping people to think critically. Unless we accept that people have views very different from ours, and that a multiplicity of interpetations of practically every idea or action is possible, we will be unable to contemplate alternatives in our own thoughts and actions.
>
> (Brookfield, 1993, pp. 238–41)

So, the conversation about the concrete experience (the difficult beginning to the lesson) might include such questions from the HOD as:

'How do you think the lesson went?'

'Why do you think that?'

'What do you think was happening at the beginning of the lesson?'

'What do you think the young people were expecting?'

As Brookfield says, the HOD cannot plan the whole conversation before it happens, and it is necessary to engage in a two-way discussion. So, the HOD also will not know the answers before the conversation begins. But it might be helpful to prepare some non-judgemental questions before the discussion begins, in order to begin the critical discussion. These questions help the NQT to think about an uncomfortable experience in a way that dissolves some of the discomfort and that develops a vocabulary which encourages objective observation. They are then more able to distance themselves from the uncomfortable feelings so that they can try to understand what was really happening.

3   **The abstract conceptualization stage** is when the vocabulary to encourage objective observation is extended by reading and talking about the theoretical frameworks which explain what really happened. In other words, the HOD might suggest some books which describe research and writing about classroom management. Or the conversation might be about learning and teaching, with reference to some psychological theories about the locus of control in classroom interactions. Readings about labelling young people as marginalized and 'deviant' might help the NQT to resist blaming, and to withstand the temptation to withdraw

attention from disturbing young people. Some schools and local authorities run courses at this stage in the careers of their new teachers, so that they can support each other while they find enough reflective space away from difficult feelings in order to understand objectively what was happening.

4   **The stage of active experimentation** is when plans are made to avoid the problems experienced originally, next time. The NQT, alone with the HOD, or in a group of other teachers, develops strategies to start lessons more effectively in the future. Because of the reflection and the reading, there will be a clearer understanding of the difficulties and their causes. It may be that the teacher decides to arrive before the class next time, or that knowledge about the counter-productiveness of shouting at young people has been developed during the abstract conceptualization stage. Whatever the plans, the NQT will go back to begin the class feeling much more confident because of going through the stages in experiential learning, and by having strategies ready for difficult times.

5   And back again to the **concrete experience**, when hopefully the same problems will not arise, but if they do, the NQT will understand better what is happening and why.

6   And the HOD will once again help the **reflective observation** stage by asking, after the lesson, how it went this time, and why.

So, rather than work in the abstract on classroom management, this new teacher has developed important coping strategies based on real experiences. They have been developed through a real understanding of what was happening, without blame, and in a way that can be used many times. And they have been developed together with another, more experienced teacher acting as a mentor. Donald Schön has written several gentle books about developing the reflective practitioner: his thesis is that most professionals can be helped to develop their professional skills by what he calls a 'practicum'.

> My design for a coherent professional school places a reflective practicum at the center, as a bridge between the worlds of university and practice. (p. 309)
>
> A reflective practicum must establish its own traditions, not only those associated with project types, formats, media, tools, and materials but also those embodying expectations for the interactions of coach and student. Its traditions must include its characteristic language, its repertoire of precedents and exemplars, and its distinctive appreciative system. And the last, if the argument of the previous section is correct, must include values and norms conducive to reciprocal, public reflection on understandings and feelings usually kept private and tacit .... . It must cultivate activities that connect the knowing – and reflection-in-action of competent practitioners to the theories and techniques taught as professional knowledge in academic courses.
>
> (Schön, 1987, pp. 311–12)

Theories and strategies for professional development are more effective when based on practice, preferably the practice of the learner. The teacher, in this case the Head of Department, is not a formal lecturer who is talking in abstract ways, but a critical friend or mentor who asks careful, well-tuned questions, and points the learner in the direction of more knowledge and understanding, at exactly the right time. Those theories are used to develop strategies which help avoid the original problems.

A form of professional development that goes on all the time in good schools and with good teachers has just been described. The profound conversations which support new teachers through some of their most intense learning curves take place in corridors, in the staffroom, in meetings and working parties, while visiting the lavatories and at the lunch table. In a learning school, they are part of the atmosphere and add to the energy of the organization. Indeed, these intense conversations which include mentoring, reflection, and references to reading and research are not only for new teachers – part of the professionalism of actively 'learning' teachers is that all are engaged in this way. Heads of Department continue to learn and to make use of mentors both for their own development and as role models for those with whom they work.

The second concept in the list on page 49 – staff development as a furtive or individualistic activity – returns to John Adair's diagram, and links professional development into school development (see Figure 2.3).

In many schools there is a professional development committee or a

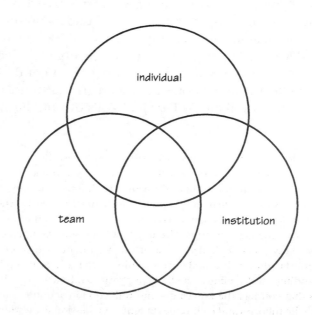

Figure 2.3 Balancing needs – professional development

member of the Senior Management Team with responsibility for professional development, whose responsibility it is to encourage professional development in the school. Maintaining the balance between the needs of the individual, the team and the institution is a driving force here – when resources are scarce this balance of needs may be an important criterion in making decisions about the sharing out of time and money. Another principle criterion is the linkage between the institutional development plan and the professional development plan. In an ideal situation, the targets, or outcomes, from appraisal are fed into both development plans, and future professional development is informed by those targets. Members of staff will automatically be encouraged to take part in the 'learning' atmosphere, and will not feel shy about asking for strategies and resources to develop professionally.

Heads of Department may be consulted about whole-school plans for professional development, but will have responsibility for creating a learning atmosphere within their departments. Exciting and productive meetings may involve learning conversations, and will include time for reflection and clarification. They will also allow for silences and uncertainties – some people need time to think about their uncertainty, and encouragement to take risks in order to learn effectively.

And so, back to effective professional development. Teachers in particular are experts in learning and teaching – they know how children learn. But they often divorce young people's learning from their own learning. As they get older, they have more memories of the uncomfortable side of learning – the risk-taking. They remember that learning can be intensely exhilarating, but it can also be incredibly uncomfortable. We all have some memory of the equivalent of learning to fly – we have held our breath and jumped without knowing if we were going to swoop or soar. Good teachers know how to help young people to soar, and to 'hold' them but encourage them while they take a breath and jump. Thus they know how skilful the teacher must be in order to make it safe enough to jump. And as we become more experienced teachers, we find it more difficult to trust other people to hold *us* while we jump, because we understand better what can go wrong.

Ideas about effective adult learning which are based on the premise that in order to take the 'learning' risk, the learner must not feel powerless or disempowered, are very appealing and make a lot of sense. Suggested Activity 16 provides further exploration of ideas about power.

When we do this exercise with participants on our courses, they invariably remember their membership of a planning group or a curriculum team or a working party as their most productive adult learning. They also talk about support groups and mentors (or critical friends). All these experiences suggest that the most effective professional learning takes place with other people or in an unthreatening atmosphere, when the learner feels powerful and ready to leap, not disempowered and afraid of falling.

Suggested Activity 16

1   Think about a time when you were excited and exhilarated by learning something professionally. In other words, you learnt something really important about learning, teaching or managing, and it has stayed with you ever since.

2   Try to draw whether you felt powerful or not when you began that piece of learning. It might be helpful here to draw a simple balance or see-saw, and put yourself on it as you began the learning:

3   Was the power shared between you and those who were responsible for your acute learning? Were you balanced, tipped down and disempowered on the balance, or pushed up by the experience and empowered?

It is usually helpful to think about our own learning when we wish to encourage it in others. When you thought about your own successful professional learning, and put yourself on the balance, you probably drew yourself *in* balance – even or perhaps up and empowered. On the whole successful learning does not take place when people feel powerless or disempowered.

It is also important, as a Head of Department, to return to another question in the list on page 48 – who is included in the term 'staff development'? Are all the members of the team teachers, or does it include classroom assistants, technicians, librarians, administrators, or support teachers? In some schools, these people are the longest serving members of staff, and often they have specially productive relationships with the young people. What about *their* professional development – whose responsibility is it? Are they included in the *learning conversations*, and might they have the opportunity to attend courses outside school? I have known laboratory technicians who have worked for part-time degrees, then followed teacher-training courses, and have subsequently returned to school as most successful teachers.

Creating a climate conducive to continuous professional development

What can be done to make sure that a Head of Department can create and sustain the appropriate atmosphere to support and encourage colleagues while they take risks? It might make this question clearer if it is articulated more carefully that there are various subsets of teachers within a department for whose development the Head of Department takes responsibility. The members of the different subsets are at different stages in their development as teachers or workers in education, and they have different needs: they include those who are thinking about promotion within or outside the school; those who are developing their professional skills and are at different growth points (they may have been teaching for twenty years and are seeking ways of remaining fresh in their work); those who are newly qualified; and those who are just entering the profession and are learning to teach within the department.

It is also necessary to continue to think about the Head of Department's own professional development. In some ways, links with institutions of Higher Education and with the Teacher Training Agency validate professional development for the Head of Department – links are maintained and a discourse of professional development is framed and maintained. Expertise is exchanged and validated, and the rest of the department have access to a valuable model of continuing development.

Although it is sometimes difficult to manage all the different demands of people at such disparate stages in their teaching careers, there are some common elements in an atmosphere which is conducive generally to professional development. In order to explore further, it is important to think about your present school climate, and the connection between what happens in the school in general and in your department in particular. Suggested Activity 17 might help clarify those common elements.

Suggested Activity 17

Next to each statement, rate the extent to which your school adopts each of these approaches as follows.
   The scoring is:
            5 = very extensively, 4 = extensively,
                3 = to a small extent,
            2 = very rarely, 1 = never

                                                                    Score

1   Staff have opportunities for the development of   ☐
     leadership through the exercise of responsibility.

2   Staff are helped to develop problem-solving and   ☐
     decision-making skills.

3   Staff participate in decision-making on significant issues   ☐
     which affect them.

4   Staff interaction and communication are facilitated by   ☐
     organizational structures and processes.

5   Staff are encouraged to experiment and initiate change.   ☐

---

6   Staff are encouraged to exchange ideas and information. ☐

7   Staff are given a clear understanding of roles and responsibilities. ☐

8   Staff are given a clear understanding of school objectives and policies. ☐

9   Staff ability to accept new challenges and experiences is developed. ☐

10   Staff have opportunities to communicate their problems. ☐

11   Staff engage in self-evaluation of school effectiveness. ☐

12   Staff contributions, opinions, values, feelings and needs are fully recognized and respected. ☐

13   Staff are encouraged and given opportunities to participate in in-service education. ☐

14   Staff evaluation is used primarily as a means towards self-evaluation and self-direction. ☐

15   Staff meetings are used as a means of co-operative problem-solving and shared decision-making. ☐

16   Staff working parties plan and experiment with new projects. ☐

17   The school acts as an agent of in-service education for the staff. ☐

18   Staff are given a sense of purpose and commitment to common goals. ☐

19   There is a carefully planned programme of induction and guidance for new teachers. ☐

20   Staff talents are discovered and fully utilized and they are able to develop their special interests. ☐

21   Important decisions and responsibilities are delegated to staff. ☐

22   Staff are given a sense of professional worth, self-respect and achievement. ☐

23   Staff are fully consulted before the introduction of changes. ☐

24   The general climate of the school encourages openness, security and trust. ☐

25   Staff are helped to realize their professional career aspirations. ☐

Source: Michael Marland (ed.) (1986) *School Management Skills*

The statements in the above activity are a reminder about a basic philosophical underpinning to professional development:

- the emphasis is on development, not training;

- development is most effective when sharing decision-making and power;
- learning schools recognize that regular talk about teaching and learning is important;
- school aims and objectives are clear and shared and are linked with professional development plans;
- successful professional development takes place all the time and at all stages of the career ladder for those who work in schools.

What can a Head of Department do to encourage these values internally?

There are some key ideas which might be highlighted in order to offer concrete suggestions. They are all well known in relation to the young people in school – any effective classroom work incorporates all the following suggestions. But they are forgotten too easily when teachers think about their own learning or that of their colleagues.

In order to encourage professional development, it is important to plan for the learner's active participation. Straightforward lectures or pieces of academic reading, without the intercession of a discussion or without a point at which small groups of people argue about how they can apply the theory to their practice, dissolve very quickly and soon become too difficult to recall. Even superb lectures given by famous and charismatic speakers eventually remain in the listener's mind as wonderful lectures or performances – the content is far more difficult to remember without a time for discussion during or immediately after the lecture. Basic psychological descriptions of learning show that learners need to talk, act, write and hear about new material in order to internalize it. Planning groups, group discussions, group tasks like some of those printed in this book, and case studies examined in small groups, all help to make learning active.

It is necessary to acknowledge and respect the learner's professional experience. One of the problems with many off-site courses and lectures is that they do not begin from the teacher/learner's experience. Those course providers who base their activities on their participants' experience are showing a respect for that experience. And people learn more when they feel that they are shown respect. They can also take the opportunity to ensure that the learning and teaching is relevant to their own needs and experience. If their own work background is acknowledged, and the learning offered begins from their own experience, relevance is assured.

The learning must be planned in a set of activities which includes reflection on experience and *access to theoretical frameworks.* It is not enough to ask people just to reflect on their experience. After a time as effective teachers, they learn how to reflect. In order to help them to move on to making plans for change, it is necessary to offer relevant readings and research findings which might illuminate and explain their experiences. Thus they are given an opportunity to articulate intellectually that which they might well know intuitively. On being offered theoretical frameworks in this way, learners are more able to make sense of their experiences in order to plan for change in their practice.

Critical thinking encourages reflective practice, in a blame and guilt free mode. It is difficult to reflect on professional activities of which the learner is ashamed. Too much is denied in order to hide from the pain of making mistakes or being involved in failure. So it is necessary to develop a careful way of talking and thinking about teaching and classroom practices which eradicates guilt. Productive critical conversations take time, and must not be too directive or judgemental.

It is important to build up a safe environment in order to encourage risk-taking. This is closely connected to the last point. If mistakes are unacceptable and always carry penalties of blame and guilt, risk-taking is impossible. If mistakes are used as bases to develop more successful strategies, and are always seen as foundations for positive learning – 'What can we learn from this?' – risk-taking is recognized as worthwhile and to be encouraged. Learners are not teased or laughed at as they try out new strategies, and they are warmly encouraged and praised for trying and learning from that trial, not just for succeeding.

Effective learning takes place when the learner feels empowered. Different people take different journeys to become effective teachers and learners. Along that journey, they have times when they are excited and successful and they come to know times when they are in pain and have a sense of failure. Heads of Department who know something of the journey undertaken by their colleagues are more able to encourage where necessary, and to understand hesitation. They learn the signs which show when their colleagues are feeling effective, and they learn to understand the silences which exist in any critical conversation.

The appraisal system as an example of staff development

There is a great deal written about appraisal, both within education and outside it. This is not the place to describe the appraisal process as it is at the moment, or to evaluate it. It is at different stages in schools all over Britain, and much has been written about the processes involved. For more information about teacher appraisal, for reports of research on the appraisal process, and for commentary on the way appraisal fits into British education at the moment, it is advisable to read the works of Professor Ted Wragg (1987, 1994).

It is possible, however, to write about the developmental underpinning of an appraisal process which is based on a belief that appraisal is a vital part of professional development. It may be that this is becoming a luxury, partly because it is too costly of time, and partly because it depends too heavily on acknowledged power-sharing between appraisers and appraisees. Indeed, in

1997 the then Secretary of State for Education demanded that the appraisal system should be 'strengthened' and that there should be rewards for performance related pay linked to target setting. An appraisal process developed on this basis would divest it of all possibility to offer individual professional development. This would be an enormous pity because suggestions for a universal appraisal system in education were initially greeted by teachers' unions and those who were committed to professional development with excitement and expectant anticipation.

In its initial planning stage, appraisal in education was developed as a way of encouraging all teachers to think about their professional practice within a non-threatening and supportive framework. Early appraisal processes seemed to be expensive of time, but to be informed by a clear understanding of effective professional development, adult learning and climates conducive to self-development. Heads of Department will probably have key roles in any appraisal system in the future, so it is important that they understand the dynamics of the process in order to keep the central links with staff development.

There are several stages in the process which are designed to guarantee that appraisees have equal power in the transactions and, where possible, are encouraged to negotiate conditions which allow them true self-appraisal and professional development. An understanding of the power balances at these stages will ensure that professional development will take place. They include:

- *Confidentiality*. Only a summary of the *agreed* targets is passed on to the Headteacher and Chair of Governors by the Head of Department. Thus a sense of safety is ensured in the interview; the Head of Department will not talk to anyone else about the fears and expectations raised by the appraisee and so the latter feels safer to explore all issues about professional practice.
- A *limited choice of appraiser*. It should be possible to ask for another appraiser if the appraisee is not happy with the appointed one. In this way, hidden agendas and long-term personality differences will not cloud the process, and the appraisee will have the opportunity to choose someone with whom they can work, and preferably who fully understands the professional activities with which they are involved.
- *Attention paid to the 'space' (time and place) for the appraisal dialogues*. A mutually agreed space is to be chosen, one which is at least as comfortable for the appraisee as for the appraiser. There are suggestions for the placing of chairs, for the silencing of telephones and for the closing of doors, all of which ensure that the appraisee is interviewed carefully without interruptions, and in such an atmosphere that enough time and careful listening are allotted.

- *Negotiated classroom observation.* If this part of the process is handled really well, the appraisee will have an ideal opportunity for clear and professional feedback about teaching. The feedback will be non-judgemental but encouraging, highlighting areas to be developed, and will be on an aspect of teaching chosen by the appraisee.
- *Negotiated targets.* The professional development targets framed as an outcome of the classroom observation and the interview will not be dictated, but will be negotiated and mutually agreed. Only after this careful process will they be recorded and transmitted without names to senior management.
- *Joint training.* When appraisers and appraisees receive appraisal training together, there is no opportunity for secrecy or for alternative plans and arrangements. There will be no hidden agendas, and the appraisee will know what can be expected of the process.

It is important to protect as many of the parts of the process as possible which enable and empower teachers to talk freely with those who manage them. Schools are necessarily hierachical and there are too few planned opportunities for this interaction. If appraisal becomes linked with pay and performance, the whole developmental nature of the transaction will disappear as teachers become concerned to safeguard their jobs and pay.

Meetings

Many teachers are puzzled by the number of meetings they are expected to attend. They see their main function in schools as working with the young people to ensure effective learning and teaching. They are required to perform many activities to support the learning and teaching, some of which they value, but many of which they are bored, de-skilled or mystified by. People are more likely to take part in an activity when they can see why it is taking place, and effective managers who understand this are more likely to make the purpose more transparent. So it is important to be clear about the reasons for the meetings which Heads of Department and their colleagues are expected to attend.

Meetings are held for many purposes, including:

- the exchange of information
- decision-making
- professional development
- planning
- consultation
- team building.

All these aims, and more, are perfectly sound. However it is important for those taking part, and especially the Chair of the meeting, to know which processes and outcomes are planned for and expected. People attending meetings need to know whether they are being passed information, whether they are expected to take part in a discussion, and whether important conclusions are to be reached, and certain outcomes agreed by the end of the meeting.

Heads of Department take part in many meetings during a working week, and they may be in a different position of responsibility within each meeting. Some meetings will be their principle responsibility; in some, they will be among a peer group; in others, they might well be the least influential member of staff; and some will include the whole staff, where they will probably be in the middle, structurally. It is possible to have most influence overtly over the meetings for which the Chair has principle responsibility, and perhaps only micropolitical influence over those in which they are least important.

The meetings a Head of Department attends will include:

- whole staff meetings
- parents' meetings
- possibly governors' meetings
- union or teacher association meetings
- departmental meetings
- working parties
- planning groups
- Heads of Department meetings
- faculty or cluster meetings
- pastoral meetings.

Each meeting will have a different purpose, a different client group and a different style. But it will be the Head of Department's responsibility to attend most of them, and to make a useful contribution, either in their own capacity or as the representative of others, because of their position as a middle manager in a school. Some schools, either by design or by 'history' have developed a format for meetings that changes only slightly for each constituency.

Planning meetings

Suggested Activity 18 includes a set of questions to clarify the different purposes of school meetings.

It is possible to see by this set of questions that there are particularly important values affecting the way meetings are planned. Meetings are among the most visible ways that those with management responsibility transmit their philosophy and beliefs about democracy to those they manage. It is easy to see the manager's underpinning values by applying these questions to meetings attended: are the meetings to be places where people can say what they think, and be heard? Or are they to be where they are told

Suggested Activity 18

It will be helpful to develop with your school, or within your department, a set of questions about meetings in which you are regularly involved and for which you have overall responsibility. They might include:

1 Is this meeting really necessary?
2 Who needs to attend it?
3 What is the purpose of the meeting – decision-making, giving information, consciousness raising, and so on?
4 What sort of outcomes do I want – will it be all right if I do not agree with the final decision?
5 Do I intend to use the meeting to listen to my colleagues' ideas?
6 If this meeting is to be truly democratic, how will I ensure that everyone is heard?
7 If I intend the meeting to be information giving and *not* democratic and decision-making, how will I make sure that everyone understands this, and how will I deal with any displeasure and misgivings?
8 Where should it take place? How long should it last? Shall I provide refreshments?
9 Any other important points relevant to your own particular situation?
10 ?
11 ?
12 ?

what to do? They might well be places where people think that they are being heard, but where in fact they are being skilfully manipulated into doing something that they had not originally wished to do.

These beliefs will also be apparent in the way the meeting is planned. Another set of questions might include:

1 Who has access to the agenda? Who sees it before the meeting? Who can add items to the agenda?
2 Who is to receive minutes of the previous meeting? How accurate are they, and who wrote them?
3 How long before the meeting takes place is the relevant paperwork accessible to those involved – agenda, minutes, and papers to be tabled?

In other words, are the participants of the meeting fully prepared to attend it? Have they had the opportunity to do the reading and 'homework' that will ensure that they know what is happening, and will they be informed enough to help make useful decisions and contributions? Will they be briefed well enough before the meeting to take part in it? Will they be able to take an active part and not be silenced?

Running meetings

Each meeting may well have a different level of formality and therefore a different process. The formality of the meeting depends on the size, the required outcome, the expectations set up by the school, and the Chair's belief and understanding about democratic processes. Some meetings are run very formally, invoking standing orders and requiring speakers to address remarks to the Chair and to the rest of the meeting through the Chair. Running meetings by standing orders is a way of controlling large meetings and ensuring that all those who wish to speak may have the opportunity to do so, as long as the Chair is skilled enough to run the meeting well. However, the necessary formality precludes any spontaneity – arguments do not flow, there is no time for hesitation, and only those who are articulate and quick-witted make the most of the audience that this type of meeting allows. I have often come away from such meetings with very mixed feelings: I have been amused and entertained by good speakers, but I have felt deeply frustrated because I have not felt able to join them in the discussion – I have been silenced by the formality and solemnity of the occasion, or by the speed and intensity, and I have been unable to organize my thoughts fast enough to make a useful point.

The Chair

If a meeting is to be run along consultative lines, and if the most senior person is responsible for the outcomes of the meeting, is it always necessary for the most senior teacher, or the person with most direct responsibility for the meeting, to take the chair? It is necessary here to explore the purpose or role of the Chair in a meeting. When more than two people meet with an agreed purpose and a shared understanding of the necessity for outcomes to the meeting, someone must take responsibility for the conduct of the gathering. It is necessary to make sure that:

- the meeting begins and ends on time;
- the meeting will be steered through explanation and discussion to a suitable ending;
- the purpose of the meeting is understood by all who attend;
- objectives are shared and agreed;
- everyone has a voice;
- all discussion is shared – not monoplized or overpowering;
- rational debate is the main tone;
- it is possible, if necessary, to acknowledge uncomfortable feelings;
- a rhythm of listening and speaking is achieved;

- all necessary information is available;
- a consensus is reached or attempted;
- outcomes are framed simply and clearly, and with agreement where possible;
- compromise is agreed where necessary;
- a record is made of the points for action;
- summing up occurs where required;
- the meeting draws to a suitable close.

A Chair who is able to pay attention to all the issues listed above is focusing on the process rather than the content. And it is absolutely necessary for a successful meeting that someone takes responsibility for that process. This is the case against those who have most invested in particular outcomes taking the role of Chair. One cannot argue persuasively and become engaged in the discourse if one is holding the whole gathering safe, and making sure that everyone is heard and that everyone has a voice. The job of Chair, paying attention to the process, is more than full-time – it is not really possible to sway and influence people while attempting to 'look after them'.

This is an excellent argument for rotating the post of Chair at each meeting. It is also an ideal activity to foster professional development. Colleagues soon learn how to chair in an enabling and empowering fashion, and they become far more tolerant of the needs of other colleagues in meetings. Those teams who customarily rotate the chair at meetings have found that their meetings have become more democratic and more productive, and that they work together as a team much more successfully. Indeed, former saboteurs of meetings quickly reform and enter into the spirit of the meetings because their turn as chair gave them a clearer stake in the outcomes of the meetings.

If the role of Chair cannot be rotated regularly, and if the person with most responsibility for the positive outcomes of the meeting must also chair it, it may be advisable to pass over the chairing of parts of the meeting, especially when an intense discussion is about to happen, or where a vital point must be won. At such times, the Head of Department must be able to concentrate on content rather than process.

The minute-taker

Nobody ever becomes a minute-taker by choice. It is an apparently thankless task which often takes hours after the end of a meeting to complete. The minute-taker is silenced during the meeting because of the necessity to write; and few colleagues read lengthy minutes once they are produced. Teams which are lucky enough to have secretarial support often ask the secretary to take the minutes. In this way, it is shown to be a demeaning job which is to be done by someone who can be spared from participation in the discussion. And yet minute taking is ultimately the most powerful position. The minutes tell the story of a meeting, and because they are usually the only record, some people write them in such a way as to change decisions made. How often have you read the minutes of a meeting you attended, and found it difficult to recognize the reported discussion? And the agreed outcomes and action to be taken often appear to be new information!

On our courses, when exploring issues about teams, teambuilding and meetings, we suggest that the minute-taker, or scribe, writes agreed notes, in front of the team. We provide flipcharts, and the scribe writes the outcomes, or agreements, of the meeting, not a verbatim report, as it is happening. In this way, those present at the meeting can see and thus agree what is to be written – only action points are written down. The scribe can participate in the discussion because the task is less onerous; and most of the work is done during the meeting – only one or two sheets of flipchart paper are to be transcribed (some schools have a machine capable of reproducing A4 notes from a sheet of flipchart paper). The added benefits are that it is easier to clarify the discussion, and to see as well as to hear the points listed as they are agreed.

Other participants

Many people find attending meetings intimidating, especially when joining one for the first time. There are ways of making meetings less intimidating, and much of the responsibility for feeling more effective in meetings lies with the people who attend them. There are some basic guidelines which may be useful, especially when a participant is representing a constituency which requires them to make uncomfortable points, or which believes that it is never heard clearly.

It is important to read the necessary paperwork before the meeting. In this way, clarification may be requested from key people before the meeting, but the representative is also ready to challenge or support where necessary during the meeting. Papers annotated with highlighter pens and notes allow a participant to be ready with relevant arguments and questions as each point is raised. If the papers are not delivered in the order in which they are to be read at the meeting, the recipient can put them in the order of the agenda, marking clearly which paper goes with which agenda item.

It is advisable to keep all papers from each meeting in files relevant to that set of meetings. Then the file can be taken to the meeting, with the possibility of referring to previous appropriate discussions, and the participant is less likely to lose the papers after the meeting!

If someone who is to take part in an important meeting tends to feel intimidated during meetings, or if they have been asked by their constituency to raise difficult issues, it is advisable to try to ask questions in role. In that way, it can be felt that choices can be made about not asking uncomfortable questions as a 'naughty' or 'difficult' newcomer, but as a dignified and thoughtful representative of several other important and professional colleagues. Indeed, it is sometimes helpful to practice questions before a meeting, with sympathetic friends, and to plan as much of the arguments as possible in preparation.

Meetings – a summary

To summarize about one of the most visible management activities, if it is accepted that a meeting is necessary then these are some of the pointers to a successful meeting.

- The purpose of the meeting should be clear to all before it begins.
- The structure and content of the meeting should be clear to all before it begins.
- The meeting will be run in such a way as to achieve the expected outcomes.
- The meeting will not necessarily be chaired by the team leader – chairing a meeting is excellent professional development.
- The meeting will be organized in such a way as to give everyone attending a voice. Strategies for sharing information before and during the meeting are helpful, and a facilitative chair will ensure that people who are slow at taking the floor are encouraged to speak, and those who talk too much are tactfully quietened.
- The agenda, compiled with open access, will be available to all concerned before the meeting.
- Papers for the meeting will be circulated early in order to give people enough time to prepare for the meeting.
- The meeting will begin and end on time, and the time will be spent purposefully, facilitated by a chair whose sole responsibility is to pay attention to the process of the meeting.
- Agreed action points and other relevant agreements will be minuted briefly and succinctly, and circulated shortly after the meeting.
- The agenda for the next meeting will take into account the action points, the agreed points, and any relevant information from this meeting.

Addressing meetings

I am always surprised by the number of middle and senior managers in schools who attend our courses and who appear reluctant to speak to the whole group in which they are working. Our groups are never larger than twenty people, and very few school classes these days hold fewer than twenty young people. I suspect that fear causes the reluctance, and that the fear is one common to many teachers – a fear of being found out, of being seen not to know the answer, and of appearing witless. And yet these are teachers who regularly work with several different classes of young people each day. There seems to be an appreciable difference between holding the attention of a class of adolescents and talking informatively to a group of adults who share the same professional interests.

Indeed, I have vivid memories of the most difficult meetings I addressed professionally. When I was a school teacher, my earliest sessions of leading assemblies with the school in which I worked (650 young people and staff) were preceded by several weeks of preparation (over-preparation), and several nights without sleep. The fear of 'drying' woke me up in panic several times. And I would only volunteer to take an assembly when I had the foundations of an idea for a session firmly embedded in my consciousness. Despite my panics, I continued to plan and deliver assemblies not for religious reasons, but because I finally came to love the sense of performance and audience that I felt, and the adrenalin rush after it went well that helped me sail through a morning of the most difficult teaching. I had the same intense mixture of feelings when I attended staff meetings in a school with about seventy-five members of staff who met together once each term.

I did not have stage fright when teaching, and I was not overcome with fear when preparing my lessons. The fears came when I thought about addressing an 'audience' of vastly mixed experience and expectations – staff *and* young people, or when planning to talk to people (the whole staff) I was not used to addressing at that stage in my career. These are two separate but equally important points:

- a fear that I would not be able to find a universally appealing subject, and once I found it,
- my suspicion that I would not be able to talk about it in a language and with references which would be understood by everyone listening.

Young people who are socially adept learn to speak several different dialects, including those of home, of their friends, of formal school interactions and of less formal school interactions with their peer group. The most socially adept of them learn to speak all these dialects without patronizing or puzzling the people with whom they speak. They appear to be able to enter several different discourses within one institution, and are able to choose the right one for the right occasion without difficulty. However, many teachers seem to lose that ease on attaining adulthood, and they often talk to everyone within the school in exactly the same tones. Indeed, teachers' styles of speech are some of the most frequently caricatured aspects of the teasing between teachers and young people.

Nonetheless, it is clear that many teachers use language as a barrier to protect themselves from those who criticize them. Some teaching colleagues speaking in public or to large groups of young people are quite likely, perhaps unconsciously, to use language as a form of control. They protect their professionalism by clothing their activities in a language that is full of codes. These codes signal who holds the cultural capital – who speaks and understands enough of the education jargon to be able to enter into an even and informed discussion with teachers. Jargon symbolizes knowledge and power, and can easily be used to silence those who do not understand the significance of the language.

So, it is important to be clear when addressing a meeting that the language to be used is to include and not exclude those who are being addressed. This is another moral issue – a balanced, two-sided discussion is a way to encourage both feedback and support, and to ensure that a school really does reflect the views of its community. So it is necessary to make sure that the language is not veiled in jargon and professional allusions, but is clear and simple without being patronizing.

All effective teachers know almost instinctively that people understand and learn best when information is communicated to them by more than one sense. In other words, when addressing any group of people in an information giving or gathering or decision-taking meeting, it is advisable to use visual aids, however simple. Key words might be written before on an overhead transparency, or on a board at the front of the room; an annotated agenda with key words and a glossary may be given out at the meeting; flipcharts are important tools, because sheets of flipchart paper are useful ways of recording suggestions, and they can be left visible to the group when the discussion moves on.

Teachers who have excellent classroom skills become tongue-tied and inaudible when they are expected to address a room of adults. And even if they are audible, they tend to speak so fast that it is almost impossible to distinguish what they are saying. Nerves often make novice public speakers breathless, and eye contact is avoided by those who are embarassed to be seen and heard in public.

A public speaker must first decide why it is necessary to speak: if it is to inform, then the speaking must be welcoming, accessible, and easily heard. If it is to ask for information or permission, then it must be all of the former, and must make it clear that interaction and response are welcome.

Then, if stage fright stops the clear calm delivery of an impromptu and virtuoso speech (and not many people can manage that), it might be as well to take time before to prepare the talk carefully, with visual aids to break up the monotony of the spoken voice. It is advisable to check that all machines are working before the session, and that the speaker knows how to use them. Loudspeakers and microphones can distort voices surprisingly, so practice in the empty room before the session can be helpful.

If good planning and carefully prepared visual aids still do not allay fears, it might help to decide to address the audience in role. Speakers persuade themselves that they are clear and careful speakers, and that they have something important to tell people. They walk slowly to where they are going to speak, they take some slow and deep breaths while looking carefully at those around them, and then they begin confidently. And they will begin to feel more confident as they proceed. They sometimes need a reminder to speak slowly and clearly, making important points verbally *and* visually, and not to be afraid of silence if they ask for responses at the end. If they have spoken well, their listeners will be engrossed in their speaking, and will need time to make sense of it. They then need to formulate their questions, and will probably be feeling at least as uncomfortable as the initial speaker when speaking in public.

Working with governors and parents

Some schools and teachers still have a great deal of work to do to build productive and trusting relationships with parents and governors. British educationists are only beginning to understand the importance of recognizing and learning from the community in which they work. Historically, parents and governors have been kept at a protective distance from schools – teachers have tried to keep the power of decision-making about educational matters to themselves, seeing it as a professional activity. But this is now not only illegal, it is recognized as a waste of powerful and dynamic resources. Morally, too, it may be seen as an unworthy attempt to divorce young people from their communities.

The separation of teachers from other interested adults grew out of the tension between teachers and other adults about the efficacy of education in this country. Teachers are in a unique position professionally in that they prepare and develop their professional expertise over many years, but because all adults have been through at least eleven years of schooling, everyone is expert in *receiving* schooling. Thus criticism of teachers' work is made by people who have a very important but partial experience of the work of teachers. Everyone has intense but particular experience of teachers' work, and it is easy to generalize from that particular experience.

The two groups of non-educator adults most involved in the work of teachers are parents and governors. Parents obviously have a great stake in the outcomes of schools, and are both members of the community in which the school is situated and 'consumers' in that they are usually closely and intensely affected by the activities of the school. Governors are also stakeholders, but usually at a greater distance from the school than parents, unless they are parent governors. Their involvement is often political or as a way of paying back and supporting the community.

Governors have a voluntary involvement in the school – they are not paid for their services – but they have a big legal responsibility. Parents have a much more personal involvement in a school, and the performance of the school may have a real influence on their lives.

Governors

The DfEE guide *School Governors – a Guide to the Law* (DfEE, 1994) lists the following powers and duties of the governing bodies of county, controlled and special schools. They are similar in spirit to the guidelines for special, grant maintained and aided schools.

Governing Bodies: Their Powers and Duties and Relationship with the Head

- helping to establish (with the head) the aims and policies of the school, and how the standards of education can be improved;
- deciding the conduct of the school – that is, how in general terms, it should be run;
- helping to draw up (with the head and staff) the school development plan;
- helping to decide how to spend the school's budget;
- making sure that the National Curriculum and religious education are taught;
- selecting the head;
- appointing, promoting, supporting and disciplining other staff;
- acting as a link between the local community and the school;
- drawing up an action plan after an inspection, and monitoring how the plan is put into practice.

(p. 15)

Several of these powers and duties relate directly to the work of a Head of Department. The tension here might be that people who have no professional understanding of teaching and learning are involved in decision-making about school work. But they have a legal responsibility for those decisions. And they are often representatives of the local community and of the children with whom teachers work; they offer an interested, thoughtful and 'other' perspective on the Head of Department's management responsibility. They also often have particular professional expertise to make up for certain gaps in the skills of educationists: financial management, building management, knowledge about living and working with people with special educational needs, linguistic and cultural expertise, and political skills. So, it is necessary to build a shared understanding of the different roles entailed, and a mutual respect and tolerance of differences. It is an important management task to find a way of working constructively with governors.

As teachers progress through their profession (and as they get older), they find themselves far less often in positions where they do not have responsibility for proceedings, or where they are regularly ill at ease because they do not understand procedures. It was a very salutary experience for me when I did a spell on Jury Service shortly after I had been promoted to Head of Department. I realized that since I had left full-time education, I had rarely spent several consecutive full days with a group of people I had not chosen to be with, or for whom I had no responsibility. I had slowly become used to choosing with whom I spent time, or attempting to have some control over those people with whom I *had* to spend time! And because experienced teachers usually work in this way, it is easy to forget the vulnerability and silence of people who do not do so – who have, for example, no clear discourse of education to bring to an education debate. This vulnerability and silence do not allow for full participation in the discussion and could encourage mistrust and sabotage. It is important, therefore, to help governors to enter the educational discourse, while encouraging them to retain their own questioning and the expertise for which they were initially invited on to the governing body. And teachers might try to enter the discourse of a non-professional engaging with education.

We have found that it is important for participants on our courses – teachers who are managers in schools – to understand how it might feel to be a member of a governing body who has been co-opted because of membership of the local community, or because of involvement in a local business. Suggested Activity 19 is a way of encouraging that understanding.

Suggested Activity 19

Working with Governors

We have developed an activity that you might use with your team, in order to understand better some of the possible problems, and to think more carefully about how you might work with governors. Stages 3, 4 and 5 of the following activity should be written on a handout and given out to members of the team with their unlabelled envelopes.

1   Make sure that you have enough roles so that there is one for each person in your team.
Choose the roles from the following, making sure that you have a Chair:
   2 teacher governors;
   2 parent governors (one of them chairs this sub-committee);
   1 deputy head;
   2 political governors;
   1 member of the support staff, nominated as representative by support staff;
   1 local business person governor;
   a co-opted governor representing the largest ethnic minority.
(Remove a political governor if necessary, or add the bursar or another co-opted governor)

2   Write the roles clearly and large enough to be seen across the table on one side of a folded sheet of A4 paper, so that it will stand up and can be used as a nameplate. Put each of them in a plain envelope, so that they are handed round to the members of the team who cannot tell what is inside.

3   Each of you should now put your 'nameplate' in front of you, so that the other participants in the meeting know the role you represent. Make sure that everyone is clear about your role and the type of school before the meeting starts – *TUNE IN*. Don't be afraid to ask clarifying questions.

4   The task is to hold a special meeting of designated governors, teachers, and support staff to agree some guidelines (approximately six) to help governors and staff work together effectively. These recommendations are to be presented to the Governing Body for consideration as policy. This is to be a positive and constructive meeting where everyone wants a successful outcome. However, participants are requested to keep in role, remembering particularly the needs of the people they represent.

5   Begin the meeting. It will last for **30 minutes** after people have been given and have understood their roles.

6   When the 30 minutes are over, the chair or an appointed time-keeper should end the session, and then, make sure that everyone is out of role.

7   Talk about what you learnt from doing this activity about being a governor who might not be able to understand what is happening. What was it like to feel silenced? What was it like to feel powerless?

8   Return to the guidelines to help governors and staff work together effectively, that you drew up while in role. Would you add anything to these guidelines after talking about the role-play itself?

It is important not to see governors in a negative or deficient way. As well as recognizing their 'other' expertise, it is important to explore ways of attuning them to the school. Some schools have linked their governors with departments or faculties. This helps to involve governors more closely in the management of the teaching and learning in the school – they can understand more clearly how their deliberations and decisions affect what is happening in the classroom. And each department or faculty has a 'champion' on the governing body. In this way, the work of the governing body is informed by a reality based on knowledge and understanding.

If the staff of a school decide to work co-operatively with their governing body, the relationship will be productive and creative. If the relationship is one of mistrust and competition for power, it can only be time-consuming and destructive.

Parents

As expectations about accountability increase, teachers, and especially Heads of Department, talk more frequently to parents and guardians and to other involved adults about the work they and their team do. And they usually find themselves, or think that they are going to find themselves, defending their professional practice to a constituency which has a stake in their work, and an intense but often partial understanding of it. So they often expect to begin from an adversarial position, and they prepare their session by cloaking their work in a professional language which confirms some of the suspicions of those listening. Communication is not easy when one side expects to be attacked, and the other side appears to mistrust the first side.

I have written earlier about the emotional intensity surrounding learning and teaching. That emotional intensity is often multiplied for parents when they experience it again through their children's schooling. Their position is usually that of championing the rights and needs of their children. Some schools think that part of their educative task is to help parents see their children's needs within the context of the needs of other children and the school. (Back to Adair's three interlocking circles). Many times, as a pastoral head, I tried to persuade parents to balance their own children's learning needs with those of the rest of their class.

But on reflection, I am no longer sure that I was right. Who should champion a young person if not a parent? Who else knows the young person as well or understands the constraints and context which have helped to form them? I now consider myself arrogant to have assumed that I knew a young person better than a parent might know them. I regularly entered unthinkingly into the competition between parents and teachers for the souls of the young people they had in common. Many teachers construct a barrier at the school gate, and think that they know what is best for young people within the school (and often at home as well). They are ready to argue with parents and to mystify the arguments with educational jargon as a way of winning. But if schools are part of the wider society and the local community, the wishes and values of these stakeholders must help to inform the guiding principles of the school. And to some extent, the school is a mouthpiece of the local community and is there to serve it.

On the whole, staff at primary schools are more used to working productively with parents than secondary school teachers, and have gone quite a way towards exploring questions of partnership. Because the parents of primary school children are more closely involved in their children's lives, they have a more central place in the life of the school. Secondary school teachers may find it helpful to visit some of their school's feeder primary schools to see how they work with parents – noting particularly the way the teachers and parents talk to each other and the way that parents are welcomed into the work of the school. The communication will not be one-way – schools which work well with parents listen carefully to them. They have well-developed strategies such as parents' rooms and regular times for informal meetings, as well as careful systems for consulting on many issues, and being ready to follow up initiatives which begin with parents.

Heads of Department, quite apart from contact with the parents of the young people they teach, might be expected to tell substantive and prospective parents about the work of their department; they may wish to use some of their skills and interests to enhance the work they and their team do; and they may wish to work in partnership with them and indeed have them working alongside the young people in their classes. And why communicate only with parents? The wider community has much to offer its local school.

John Sayer explores this linkage further when he writes about community education:

> Those who have responsibility for significant areas of curriculum – for departments, faculties, or cross-curricular teams – have to develop the ability to negotiate school programmes in relation to community needs and alternative resources available. They have an active role in creating access to school programmes from other age groups and across schools. The co-operative community dimension has to be built in not just to job descriptions but to the way the job is seen and done.
>
> (Sayer, 1993, p. 72)

In order to work constructively and productively with parents and governors, the staff of a school will have reached an understanding about the place of their school in the community and about the importance of the voice of the community in decision-making about the school's direction and activities. Management strategies will take into account the necessity and ethical validity of the involvement of parents and governors, and these strategies will be made clear to all visitors to the school by such evidence as the way visitors are welcomed; the communication systems between home and school; the language used when parents are addressed by staff; and the presence of parents and governors in the school during the school day.

Presenting the department within the school

It is helpful here to think about how schools work structurally, and to understand the tensions about the location at which a Head of Department *leads* one team (the members of the department), *negotiates equally* within another team (either within a faculty or directly with the other Heads of Department), and *is managed by* those who have responsibility for the work of each part of the school (the Senior Management Team or its equivalent) (see Figure 2.4).

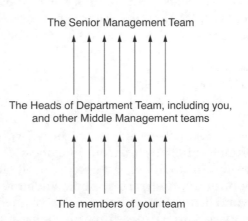

Figure 2.4　Linking the department with the rest of the school

The way the Head of Department works with this position affects the way the department is represented inside and outside the school. A Head of Department is involved in a mixture of managing and being managed, so it is necessary to operate differently with different people at any time.

Two more structural issues make a difference here:

1   A member of the Senior Management Team, or someone who manages the Head of Department, might well be a member of the team; and
2   The spirit behind the decision-making processes in the school will determine whether decisions are two-way or not – who has a voice?

Suggested Activity 20 will help further exploration of managing and being managed.

Suggested Activity 20

If you return to Suggested Activity 2 on page 3 where you were asked to draw a simple diagram of your school and your place in it, you might add some more stages to your diagram which will make the tensions clearer to you. You will need several different colours, and a large enough piece of paper to hold arrows flying in several different directions.

1   Draw the arrows between you and those for whom you have management responsibility, making the thickness or strength of the arrow signify the strength of the communication between you.

2   In another colour, draw arrows between you and those people who manage *you*, again making them stronger or thicker in relation to the strength of the communication between you.

3   In a third colour, draw in the arrows between you and those people with whom you share management responsibility – for example, other Heads of Department. Indicate the frequency and effectiveness of the communication, as before.

4   Are those arrows two-way or one-way? Are the different thicknesses of the arrows significant? Is there always negotiation, and do you have a way of informing or affecting the decisions of those who manage you?

The Head of Department is the person with the clearest understanding about managing the learning and teaching in specific subject areas, so the rest of the school will need to know about their work, and they will need to know about the work in other departments – the young people with whom the department works learn from nearly all departments within a school week. And co-operation rather than ignorance or competition models an ethical way of working together.

There are several times when a Head of Department has an important public relations role including:

- describing the work of the department to parents and young people so that they will understand why they should choose to do the specific subject for GCSE or A level;
- presenting the work of the department so that young people come to the school in order to study the specific subject with the team;
- presenting the department favourably enough to recruit the best teachers to make up the team;
- describing the work clearly enough for the OFSTED inspectors to understand and respect what is done in the department;
- listening to and negotiating with other constituent groups in the school when developing policies and making whole-school decisions;
- ensuring that informed decisions are made about resourcing the school – explaining the needs of the department while under-standing and paying attention to the needs of other departments;
- talking about the work of the department to the planners and decision-makers in the school so that it features clearly and equitably enough in school plans for the future.

So in order to promote the department, a team leader needs to understand how it fits into the whole school; they will then develop a way of describing its work clearly and attractively; they will be able to show short-, medium- and long-term planning in such a way as to show a sense of direction in the work of the department; and the Head of Department and the department team will be sure that they are answering the needs of the school, the young people and the National Curriculum when making these plans. This is an interrelating set of issues, most of which are linked by good curriculum planning, and by a departmental commitment to the agreed curriculum.

In order to promote the department, it is necessary to be clear about a communication style, which might be different depending on the con-stituents who take part in the communication. This communication style will also be informed by educational values, and by an understanding of educa-tional management. Suggested Activity 21 shows a way of exploring communication links.

This might well be a very salutary experience – middle managers are caught up in education's entry into the market place where they must sell their products, but they are still seen as teachers whose main aim is to develop the young people with whom they work, as well as they can. They are not just purveyors of wisdom and knowledge, but also formulate what counts as wisdom and knowledge, and are then engaged in transforming young people into wise and knowledgeable citizens.

Suggested Activity 21

1   Draw a 'map' of yourself and your links with the different sets of people and constituents with whom you need to talk about your department. In other words, who do you promote it to? And how are they connected to you?

2   Leave the map alone for a few days while you do your normal work around the school. But while you talk to the different sets of people, think about two main questions:

Why are you talking (are you selling, buying, or informing)?

How are you talking (what sort of language are you using and how does it make the balance of power clear)?

3   Go back to the map and find a way of marking the answers to the two questions on the links between you and the constituents.

4   Then ask yourself whether the constituents would have the same answers to the two questions as you have.

Presenting the department to the world outside

Some schools see certain departments as particularly attractive when trying to persuade prospective parents and young people that the school is worth enrolling in. Sports and performing arts specialists are used to this, but other departments such as science and mathematics are also often used as a selling point. On prospective parents' evenings and open days, teachers are encouraged to use all their presentational skills to describe their work in as attractive a way as possible. Many teachers enter into all this with a mixture of cynicism, weariness and hope.

It is important that the leader of a team of teachers has clarified, both personally and with the team, why this could be a productive activity. Quite apart from the importance of recruiting a good number and a wide range of young people who are fully representative of the local community, it is important to use the opportunity to articulate the business of the department in clear and accessible terms. Schools are often so deeply involved in their daily activities that a regular opportunity to reflect on and then to describe that activity in simple terms is very important. It serves as an occasion for team members to reaffirm their commitment to the core values and purpose of their work and then having described it to themselves, describing it to others encourages self-respect.

There are also times when a Head of Department has contact with the Press, and indeed with the media in general. Although television news coverage has evolved rapidly over the last few years in a highly competitive industry, schools have very mixed feelings about contact with the media.

Sometimes they wish to use them to represent the school in a positive light and to describe pioneering work; sometimes they wish to celebrate achievement; sometimes they hope to find a channel for campaigning; and sometimes they need coverage of a news story.

Bill Yule and I have written elsewhere about working with the media when a school has been involved in a crisis – it is important that a school should nominate a staff member to deal with the media in a crisis, and that the same person should always be informed of any activities with the Press in more peaceful times as well.

> One of the tasks of schools [after a crisis] must be to protect children, parents and staff from the glare of publicity, particularly during the first week or so. While the media can help inform the public responsibly, it can also be harmfully intrusive at times of stress and personal grief. Reporters move on to the next catastrophe; a survivor may live for years with a foolish quote in an unguarded moment.

> A senior person on the staff should be nominated as press officer to deal with the media. It is not advisable to permit press and television on to the school premises or to give them access to staff or children unless there are specific reasons for doing so. All enquiries should be directed to and through the press officer who can arrange to have a briefing session with the press if necessary (ie journalists may be invited to a particular part of the school at a specified time). If the press are aware of these arrangements, they may be less inclined to crowd the school gates or try to interview individual pupils, staff or parents. While factual information may be given to the press, the privacy of staff, young people and their families should be maintained.
>
> (Yule and Gold, 1993)

It is advisable for a Head of Department to spend some time thinking about the relationship between their department and the media. If there are no whole-school guidelines, it is as well to develop departmental guidelines. Basically, it is important to try to have some control over what is being reported. Tim Devlin and Brian Knight published a very useful book, *Public Relations and Marketing for Schools*, which gives very helpful advice, and they suggest that relationships with the media should be as systematic and professional as possible (Devlin and Knight, 1990). In *Marketing the School*, Michael Marland and Rick Rogers are very positive about the way that good marketing can help a school develop good relationships with the local community. They see that schools who manage their own publicity well can be more independent and more able to shape themselves (Marland and Rogers, 1991).

Where possible, think first about why it is necessary to involve the media, describe the relevant work as clearly and unequivocally as possible, and all the time think about the effects of this publicity about the school on the local and national community. In this way, those people who work in schools will ultimately have more control over their professional activities.

CHAPTER 3

Managing resources

Many managers in education think about 'resources' as finances, and are overawed by them: 'I came into teaching to teach, not to work with money!' But every educational aim, and every decision at any level of management, has a resource implication and must be planned for. It may well be a financial decision because time and people ultimately cost money, but there are other important implications too and these are usually educational.

Diffidence about finances is made worse by the fact that almost every school has a different system for agreeing and distributing resources. Some systems rely on teams of school-based people, and others are dependent on one key decision-maker. Local Education Authorities have developed different financial formulae, and have devolved different monies to their schools, and so some have kept more control than others over the money and attendant decision-making.

What resources?

It is important to think about what is covered by the word 'resources'. Obviously money received as the outcome of departmental bidding. But it also encompasses all the people – staff, both teaching and support staff, are the most expensive resource in any department. It also includes equipment, materials, space and facilities, which vary depending on the curriculum area, and time allotted to the department.

Resources and equity

One outcome of the changes over the last few years about school-based resources is that issues of equity which include race, class, gender and special educational needs no longer rest with local authorities. They have become the responsibility of specific schools, who have more freedom in these areas than previously. However, the resourcing of schools could become especially problematic because when there are finite resources but seemingly infinite demands made on them, views about equity are tested hard.

In 1995 Sharon Gewirtz, Stephen Ball and Richard Bowe published *Markets, Choice and Equity in Education* which described the findings of a three-year study about the effects of market forces on schools and education. They identified a number of key trends which they noted in the schools in their study which showed the effects of the market on issues of equity. Although the following summary of their findings appears initially to refer to whole schools and their relationship to their communities and to the wider context of society, there are some very important lessons here for Heads of Department to think about when bidding for the resources they offer the young people through their curriculum responsibility. These points should be remembered by those who are in the process of bidding for resources.

> 1 Concerns about image are driving schools in some instances to adopt short-term and superficial solutions to deep-seated problems which ideally require a significant investment of time and resources to resolve.
> 2 The market is encouraging schools to pass the buck of responsibility for the most socially and educationally vulnerable students and this appears to be leading to an intensification of segregation across local school systems.
> 3 Schools are introducing practices which are likely to result in increased social segregation and provisional differentiation within institutions.
> 4 The market appears to be effecting a redefinition and a narrowing of scope of schooling to exclude the social dimensions of education.
> 5 By promoting a view of schooling and children as commodities, the market may be generating a new 'hidden curriculum' of the school.
>
> (Gewirtz, Ball and Bowe, 1995)

Departmental resources

Every school has a different system for bidding for and allotting resources. It is vital that Heads of Department understand both the overt and the micropolitical systems as soon as possible, because the financial year is different from the academic year, and formal bidding cycles usually begin in the middle of the school year. In a well-organized school, the bidding cycle has a long run up to the final decision-making phase, and most of the staff will take part in it at some stage. In a less well-organized school, deadlines always arrive before staff are ready for them, and micropolitical relationships have too much influence over the decision-making processes.

Structurally, bidding systems are different in every school, and it is necessary that team leaders do not feel worried about asking for frequent explanations in order to understand the system with which they are working. If they are embarrassed about not understanding, or worried about the mathematical or financial complications, they may well remember that this is about supporting the learning and teaching in their departments, not about their own intellectual capacities! And for a new Head of Department, the differences between systems are an excellent excuse for the necessity of more explanations.

Many schools try to reflect their philosophy of education in the way management decisions are made. Thus they publish dates to all staff during the year when decisions have to be made at different stages about resourcing the work of the school. They also publish explanations of the decision-making processes, and are clear about the information necessary to inform the decision-making. This information might be a simple and universally accepted pro forma, or it might be in the form of a presentation from each Head of Department.

The final resourcing decisions are sometimes made by representative groups of staff members who process the departmental information given to them by comparing it to an agreed and published set of criteria for funding.

Numerous changes in the systems for funding schools means that the formula for the resources given to schools changes each year. And some schools change their internal bidding systems frequently. These changes mean that even well established Heads of Department have careful planning to do when thinking about bidding for resources. And it is as well to take time to make those plans well ahead of the deadlines, so that sufficient departmental meetings can be used to address the resourcing bids. Suggested Activity 22 will help to make sense of the school's resourcing plans.

Suggested Activity 22

1   At the beginning of the academic year, brainstorm with members of your department to pool information about the bidding system in your school. This will include:

– relevant school dates;
– necessary information, including relevant pupil numbers and previous bids;
– establishing the necessary and relevant paperwork;
– clarifying which people are involved in the decision-making process;
– agreeing how members of the department will make their own decisions about the bid;
– deciding which audits are necessary within your department in order to strengthen your bid – for example, what information do you have about numbers and results? (How well do you know what equipment and material can be found in your department?)

2   When the school dates for the bidding cycle are clear and agreed, put them into your school diary.

3   Plan all necessary departmental meetings, making sure that relevant information will be available at the right time, that all members of your department have those dates, that they all know what information is necessary beforehand, and that everyone is aware of what is to be achieved at each meeting.

As always, it is important to match the tone of the bid and the amount of money asked for (over that expected) with general values and beliefs in the rest of the school. Basic educational ethics about equity, about access to curricula, and about an acceptance of the developmental nature of the educational process all influence the style and amount of the bid. And it is advisable for Heads of Department to decide whether they intend to work within the accepted framework, or whether to be individualistic about their department's needs. Whichever decision they reach will also be informed by an understanding of whole-school needs and a whole-school overview of the resourcing implications. In schools where educational decisions are under-pinned by a clear philosophy of equity and entitlement, departments negotiate together rather than work for the aggrandizement of specific departments.

Because of various external influences, such as turbulence in decisions about what constitutes a National Curriculum; such as the laws about provision for children with special educational needs; and such as the Home Office's changing relationship to the support, through Section 11 funding, of bilingual learners, different departments will have become more or less prominent in the school in a very short time. In other words, some tradition-ally large and comparatively well-funded departments, with well-established bidding procedures, and large expenditures compared with the rest of the school, may well find their spending suddenly curtailed because fewer young people choose to study their subject, or because of the necessity of teaching larger classes. And other departments, such as Special Educational Needs or Learning Support, become much more central and important to the school because they bring in money directly as a result of changes in funding. They then begin rapid staff recruitment drives, and their record-keeping systems and schemes for the induction of new teachers need added and immediate resourcing.

Managing the department budget

This is another occasion when, if possible, a Head of Department approa-ches the expert for advice. There are several times when it is very helpful to be a member of a team, and if the person with ultimate management responsibility for a curriculum area has difficulties with finances and with mathematical problems, this is such a time. It is necessary for a Head of Department to understand the fundamental principles of bookkeeping, simply so that they are not mystified in such a way as to be frightened, and it is liberating to be able to work with figures if they so choose. However, it is not always necessary to set up or invent complicated systems for each department.

Many state schools now have either a Bursar or someone whose chief role it is to work with the finances of the school. *They* set up the systems, usually after consultation with staff in order to set up a relevant and workable system.

And they quickly become used to working with people who are frightened of figures and finances. Good financial advisers develop budgeting systems which can be adapted to each department in the school. They then transmit the basic principles of the system to those people who are going to use them; they monitor that they are usable and used regularly; and, hopefully, they are tactful in checking that the work is done effectively and in time. A wise Head of Department makes use of this expertise in the organization – when this relationship works well, it is an excellent example of education informing finance and vice versa.

If such an expert is not within reach, John Hart has written an approachable book, *Successful Financial Planning and Management in Schools*, which explains budgeting and financial planning in schools. It is addressed to those with whole-school responsibility, but it is as well to understand where the work of a department fits into that of the school, and there are some useful and transferrable suggestions for forms and strategies. (Hart, 1993)

Clearly it is important to know what resources the department contains, and regular audits ensure that the departmental resources are healthy. Taking into account the findings of Gewirtz, Ball and Bowe (1995), quoted earlier, departmental audits are not just about registering staffing and 'plant'. They are about understanding and supporting the fundamental work of the department. Decisions about what information to gather during an audit and how to interpret that information must be informed by a thoughtful understanding about the educational provision of *all* the young people for whose learning and teaching the departmental team has responsibility.

Les Bell, in his book *Managing Teams in Secondary Schools* (Bell, 1992), links a staffing audit with the school development plan. Gewirtz, Ball and Bowe also link resource audits with the redistribution of teachers – in their project, they looked particularly at the redeployment of learning support teachers in order to spend less on the pupil:teacher ratio. The writers of these two books see resourcing departments mainly as staffing them.

Derek Torrington and Jane Weightman, in *The Reality of School Management*, looked at the task of management in 24 maintained secondary schools. They wrote about the 'control of resources', and described the freedom to be found in well-managed resources in a school. They described a positive view of resources as those things teachers and managers in schools can control, exploit and invest, and which leads to the sense of ownership that will produce thoughtful use. It does not matter how limited the actual amounts of money, time or space are, it is the attitude to their availability and use that is important. (Torrington and Weightman, 1989)

In order to invest the auditing and sharing of resources in the department with a 'positive' attitude, it is necessary to have a clear and agreed system of audit which at the same time is easy to use. The paperwork expected of teachers in their daily work is so demanding that any added systems should be quick and easy to use, and so persuasively acceptable that their use is automatic. Liz Armstrong, writing with others, suggests some activities which help Heads of Department to draw up easy-to-use stocktaking systems (Armstrong, 1993).

Fundraising

Schools have always raised funds, but there have been times when fundraising was the responsibility of a small committee, and the spending of the funds raised was directed by that committee. The money was not central to the budgeting of the school, and it was used to buy 'extras'. Fundraising has rapidly become more necessary in schools. In some ways, this gives schools more freedom to resource themselves, but the wide disparity in the wealth of communities in which schools are situated means that there is a wide disparity in the amount of money raised. In order to erase this disparity some schools have encouraged professional fundraisers to work with them. Sometimes they employ them as consultants; sometimes they co-opt them on to governing bodies, and sometimes they are lucky enough to have them as parents.

There are some ethical issues about raising money, such as:

- Its *provenance* – how was the money made, and does it matter whether the donors are ethically sound?
- *Does the money come with strings attached* – do the donors give the money freely or do they wish to make sure that they have influence in some way over the way the money is spent or over future activities at the school?
- *Who should spend time raising money* – are teachers appointed to teach young people, or is it necessary for them to spend time in fundraising activities in order to get the resources necessary for effective teaching? Some people argue that schools should not divert the time which could be used for learning and teaching into time for fundraising.
- *Should money be raised for what were originally termed 'capital costs'* – such as staff salaries, teaching materials and building maintenance, or should schools expect these costs to be paid from central funds as a right?

However, a radical view of fundraising is that the provenance of the money is not important – it may be being 'liberated' from unethical investments, for example. What really matters is that more money is found in order to support the learning and teaching in the school. As a result, more young people will be enabled to have access to a broader curriculum.

Some young people become involved in fundraising for their schools – this can once again take away valuable learning and teaching time. But it can also encourage pride in their work and their school, help them to understand society better, and help them to understand more clearly the value of money as they raise it for their own school.

It is important to have thought through the general issues and maybe to have drawn up some guidelines together as a school on ethical fundraising. Then it is possible to begin to think about fundraising strategies. There are many sources of funding available – local, national and international – and those who understand fundraising processes are very valuable to schools.

Schools make money by fundraising activities, by seeking sponsorship, and by writing bids for funding. An ability to raise money is partly luck, partly hard work, and partly knowledge of the right places to apply. If a Head of Department has none of this knowledge, and there is no one attached to the school to help them, it might be helpful to attend a course on fundraising (local authority voluntary agencies often run such courses). Local sponsors are obviously very valuable, but there are also national grant giving bodies (there is a national register of grant giving trusts), and there are various agencies within the European Union to which educators in the UK now have access.

It is important to take time to make serious plans. Many fundraising bids (which on the whole bring in more money than fundraising activities) fail because they have not taken account of the relevant timetable, because they have not been prepared carefully enough, or because the relevant people have not been notified. It is necessary therefore to work strategically, first finding out the parameters of a bid, then checking the timetable for application, then collecting all the necessary material and producing it well in order to submit a stylish bid. Such details make a difference between success and failure, and depend on a level of commitment to the activity.

CHAPTER 4

Managing the curriculum

The curriculum

Before the 1990s, when most educationists talked about 'the Curriculum', they took pride and pleasure in finding as many ways as possible to describe what they meant. The reason for this discussion was to show that teachers must be conscious of *everything* that young people learnt when they come to school, whether intended or unintended, overt or hidden, planned as received or transmitted. Brainstorms about the curriculum, done at that time, were rich in creative thinking about the breadth and depth of the learning and teaching on offer in schools. Indeed, teachers were encouraged to take responsibility for as many aspects of the curriculum as they could.

> We feel able to state that our concern is with *all* the following:
> 1 the intended curriculum as formally stated by the timetable, in syllabuses and schemes of work, in aims, or as it exists in the general but unstated intentions of teachers;
> 2 the actual curriculum as experienced by pupils when they are involved in learning activities;
> 3 the hidden curriculum where pupils experience and 'learn' through such experiences as lining up to enter school, wearing school uniform, standing up when a teacher enters the classroom, or being locked out of the school at break and lunchtimes;
> 4 the outcome of learning in terms of the understandings, attitudes etc. that pupils develop.
> (This view of the curriculum implies that curriculum evaluation is concerned with questions about what should be taught as well as finding out what happens in the classroom.)
>
> (McCormick and James, 1983)

In recognizing that the school curriculum was one of the most important sites for engaging in and perhaps resolving the social divisiveness of the United Kingdom, it became a politically contested area. Geoff Whitty traces the moves of the major political parties in this country when playing out this contest (Whitty, 1985). So when the Conservative party introduced the National Curriculum in 1989, it was difficult for those who were involved in education to see it dispassionately. It was seen as an attempt to retain a sociological status quo.

Thus, many educationists feared that definitions of 'curriculum' would become too narrow because of the threatened emphasis on the legislated, taught, and planned curriculum. Many people feared that 'curriculum' would come to mean 'syllabus' only. These were often the teachers who had thought carefully about learning and teaching, and saw them in very broad terms. There were unfortunately other schools which already delivered a very narrow curriculum to the young people who attended, and that curriculum was often based on socially constructed choices, dictated by positions of race, class and gender and without any thoughtful intervention. It remains the responsibility of those who manage the curriculum to keep the interpretation of what is taught and learnt as wide if not wider than McCormick and James suggest, and to keep spaces for that which is not in the National Curriculum but which is seen as important by the school community.

If read in the most hopeful light, the National Curriculum could rescue the learning and teaching in some schools in at least two ways:

- the cross-curricular strands are the responsibility of every teacher in a school, and are carefully monitored by OFSTED (although other than the easily monitored strand of Information Technology, OFSTED inspections are not always strong on evidence of cross-curricular strands);
- narrowly defined subject areas might be broadened.

Indeed, to many schools, the National Curriculum offered an opportunity to redefine sclerotic old notions of 'curriculum', 'syllabus' and 'subject'. In order to see this most clearly, it is exciting to visit a well-organized primary school. Primary curriculum coordinators have engaged in careful curriculum mapping which allows them and their colleagues to identify what is taught at which Key Stage and through which discipline and medium. They have developed strategies, structures, knowledge (and almost a new language) to ensure that the young people with whom they work have access to a balanced and broadly-based curriculum. Some of these mapping strategies could be incorporated into planning activities in secondary schools, especially when keeping track of cross-curricular strands. Suggested Activity 23 offers a strategy to begin a departmental discussion about curriculum provision.

This activity is based on the premise that it is the responsibility of a Head of Department to remind the team to keep definitions of 'curriculum' as broad as possible.

Suggested Activity 23

1   With all the members of your department, brainstorm 'curriculum', reminding them that a brainstorm includes all 'off the wall' ideas, without judgement.

2   When the brainstorm has run out of steam, talk about the different suggestions, putting a ring round those for which you and your department are able to take direct responsibility.

3   Keep this brainstorm to refer to when you plan the curriculum more formally within your department. Tick off the suggestions you have ringed when you incorporate them in your planning.

Being the 'expert' in a curriculum area

In other parts of this book, I have sought to articulate the expertise necessary for curriculum leadership and to clarify the required balance between the importance of having and maintaining subject knowledge, and developing the ability to lead other teachers through the learning and teaching of that subject.

It seems clear that 'Head of Department' is a role which teachers take on with one set of skills, but while they are in the role they develop another set of skills. Although the Teacher Training Agency's Subject Leader Qualifications may eventually change this in some way, in practice Heads of Department are promoted to the post because they know a lot about learning and teaching in their subject. While doing the job they necessarily develop the management skills which help them to develop that knowledge in the rest of their team. A skimming read-through of the advertisements for Heads of Department in a current issue of *The Times Educational Supplement* shows that the most common phrases used to encourage teachers to apply for Head of Department posts are that they should be 'well-qualified and experienced'. Combined with these requests, one advertisement asks for an 'inspirational Head of English', two would like people with 'enthusiasm', and yet another would like 'energy and dynamism'. It appears from this quick piece of research that knowledge and experience are by far the most important attributes, but energy and enthusiasm might be welcome!

It is necessary for good Heads of Department to keep several different parts of their job in balance with each other:

- subject knowledge;
- pedagogical understanding – how learning and teaching can be best encouraged;
- systems and strategies for monitoring and evaluating their subject;

- knowledge and understanding of the legal frameworks for their work (the National Curriculum, SEN provision, cross-curricular strands, and so on);
- management qualities and skills;
- an understanding of the whole school and the place of the department in the school.

These are not in any hierarchical order, but it is important to think about which ones should be the chief activity and responsibility of the Head of Department, and which ones can be delegated to other members of the team. It may be that all are significant at some stage but not at the same stage. Depending on the expectations of the panel that appoints a new Head of Department, it could be understood that all curriculum leaders initially need subject and pedagogical knowledge, but they must show that they have the ability to develop the other areas as they progress in their role.

Is it necessary that curriculum leaders are always at the forefront of *subject* knowledge, or is it more important for schools that they are at the forefront of understanding about everything else on the list above? Clearly, they could ensure that some team members are at the forefront of subject knowledge, and be ready to ask them to share their expertise with everyone else.

It is important to have thought about this question and come to some conclusions for several reasons, but chiefly for professional development arguments. What is it really necessary for the team leader to generate, and what can be developed in team members? Might it not be possible that team members, especially new teachers fresh from teacher education and therefore most recently on the receipt of the most up-to-date information in the subject, can best be expected to provide subject expertise, and the leader be left to co-ordinate all the other parts of the work, as long as the Head of Department does not become hopelessly out of touch with the subject? After all, understanding about specific subjects, about the legal definitions of the subject, about the syllabus and assessment requirements and about favoured teaching methodology all change quickly and fairly often.

So courses and professional development opportunities on the actual subject might be left to other team members, and those on managing the subject could be offered to some members of the team and the team leader. A division of responsibilities is a helpful strategy for professional development. However, it is important to have an overview of recent developments in subject areas – regular reading of professional journals and *The Times Educational Supplement* help in keeping in touch with new knowledge, and some local authorities provide regular meetings for Heads of Department. It may require effort to take part in these extra-curricular activities, especially if it has been decided that some members of the department have responsibility for keeping everyone up to date with knowledge. But an overview rather than detail is necessary so that the team leader knows what they are managing and so that the team knows that the team leader knows. When we ask teachers what they want in someone who manages them, they often put 'knowledge' next to 'people skills'.

It is important to have *some* expertise in the curriculum area – the present team leader was probably the most knowledgeable person in it when they were appointed Head of Department. But other members of the department will quickly develop more expertise in different parts of the subject. It is important to retain an overview of the subject, and to remain ultimately responsible for all the work of the department. However, the team leader could encourage the development of more current knowledge in other people in the team.

Developing curriculum aims

The connections between the aims of the school and the aims of each curriculum area are important. If the links are clear to all, then the school's philosophy of education will be clear to all. Early in this book I wrote about the necessity to link school aims with curriculum aims, and I suggested an activity through which a Head of Department could develop departmental aims directly from school aims (see pages 5 to 9).

Before an examination of this process continues, it is important to explore definitions of such terms as 'aims', 'objectives', 'targets' and 'success criteria'. Planning for, teaching and assessing the National Curriculum, have all encouraged teachers to be much more comfortable with strategic planning, and they are more able to describe their learning targets and to measure whether young people achieve them. However, it has become clear, through the work we do in this area with teachers, that we all mean something slightly different when we use these terms. After years of inconclusive discussion, I have realized that this does not really matter, as long as we each use the same terms throughout each process and follow the same process with that same terminology through to its conclusion. It really is not important whether 'aims' and 'principles' mean the same thing, or whether 'objectives' and 'targets' are synonymous, as long as they are really connected to each other and the former informs the latter. What matters most is that clear and productive planning takes place, and that a process, agreed and understood by all those people who are involved in it, is followed through so that what happens in the classroom is clearly connected with the aims of the school.

Some Guidelines for Writing, Objectives, Targets and Success Criteria

Here is one set of terminology that we suggest, and a process that I hope you will find helpful. Do not become too engaged in linking the terms interchangeably with those you already use.

Take the whole process presented here, with its links and contacts, and see whether you can use it as an example of a planning strategy.

Objective setting

Objectives must be related to principles/aims; for example, one of your principles might be 'to improve equal opportunities in the class-room'.

Make your objectives as clear as possible – start with the word 'to', followed by an action word.

Objectives spell out aims more specifically so that theory can be translated into practice. For example, one objective for the aim above might be: *'to develop strategies to ensure that teachers pay enough attention to girls in class'.*

Target setting

Choose achievable targets for the stated objective. Set short-, medium- and long-term targets. Be specific here, if necessary using your diary or your calendar. Explain why these dates are appropriate. For example:

Short term: Awareness raising, e.g. by introducing staff at a meeting to the research literature which shows that boys get more attention from teachers than girls. To do this within a month in order to begin the process.

Medium term: Having agreed a checklist for appropriate classroom management, ensure regular peer monitoring to establish that improvements are taking place. Put the dates for the whole academic year in diaries to make sure that the monitoring happens.

Long term: Arrange a meeting at which a paper collating the findings from the monitoring is to be discussed. This should happen a year after the beginning of the project to evaluate its effectiveness.

Success criteria

These answer the question: 'How will I know when I have achieved my objective?'

For the above objective, these might include that the paper shows that 25 per cent more girls answer questions in class; or that the same paper shows that the monitoring has changed the practice of 75 per cent of the staff.

Suggested Activity 24 will help to put this framework into practice.

Managing Special Educational Needs

I find it hard to write a dedicated subsection about Special Educational Needs (although I was a Special Educational Needs teacher in secondary schools for twenty years) because I do not wish to marginalize issues of

---

Suggested Activity 24

If as a department or a school you do not agree with the definitions of the terms 'Objective setting', 'Target setting', or 'Success criteria' in the above Guidelines, substitute your own. Then try the activity in the Guidelines, because it takes you carefully through a useful process. Having agreed terms and looked at the process as an exercise, try it with department members on a real piece of planning.

Then return to the activity described near the beginning of this book (pp. 8–9) when the school educational philosophy was translated into departmental aims. Continue from there in small groups within your departmental team.

This work should be done in small groups of about three people. Each person should take one curricular aim/principle from the six departmental principles you drew up previously. Take it in turns to put it into context for the rest of your group.

The group should look at the principle/aim, and:
– frame not more than three objectives to achieve that aim;
– set short-, medium- and long-term targets for one objective;
– establish the success criteria for that objective.

Repeat this process for each member of the group. Divide the time between you equally so that each person will have a chance to present a curricular aim/principle.

If you have not followed this process through so logically before, you will probably find that the first time you translate a departmental aim into specific objectives, targets and success criteria, it takes so long that it seems to be an interminable procedure. But subsequently, it becomes much faster, and eventually automatic. That is when the whole activity is really helpful and productive, and all the links connect the school's aims with what actually happens in your classroom.

---

special needs into a corner of this book, much as young people with special educational needs might be marginalized within a school. I would rather the reader could see from the whole book what the main issues about Special Educational Needs might be. I hope that it is obvious that all educational planning and discussion must be informed by and suffused by notions of equity, which should include special young people.

However, there are two concepts to be explored here. One is about the access rights of all young people who are learning your subject, and the other is about a basic understanding of the legal requirements for the provision of special education for all those who need it, within your curriculum area.

Basic rights

Young people with special educational needs have the basic right to equality of opportunity. Just as in issues of race, class and gender, curriculum planners should automatically pay attention to giving access to a balanced and broadly-based curriculum to young people who have special educational needs. It is not always easy to remember special young people when there are pressures about such indicators as league tables – John Fish and Jennifer Evans in *Managing Special Education* (Fish and Evans, 1995) remind us that the search for higher standards has resulted in little attention being paid to developing a rationale to meeting the needs of young people who are harder to teach. There is another reason for ensuring that educational philosophy of your school is translated into your curriculum aims – most schools' professed attention to achieving potential can be put into practice for people with special educational needs in this way.

There can be a temptation among busy subject teachers to leave special young people to specialist teachers. It is important to understand that experts in Special Education are people who understand about special ways of learning and teaching, but they rarely have all the relevant subject knowledge. They can be most usefully employed during curriculum and lesson planning – their expertise, combined with subject knowledge and expertise, can ensure full access to the planned curriculum. Schools which have large and active Special Educational Needs departments have many different ways of organizing provision but it always necessitates effective liaison between the Heads of the two departments.

Legal requirements

John Fish and Jennifer Evans write that the Education Act 1993 statutory regulations and the SEN Code of Practice set out the framework for special education. The Code, *Code of Practice on the Identification and Assessment of Special Educational Needs* (DFE, 1994), has five sections:

- Section One stresses integration, intervention and partnership and sets out the fundamental principles on which the Code is based. It addresses the necessity of appropriate provision and suggests that most frequently this will be within a mainstream school.
- Section Two sets out definitions, the responsibilities of governors and the school-based stages of assessment and provision, including in-school and external specialist support.
- Section Three sets out procedures for the statutory assessment of special educational needs, showing the links with the LEA, and assuming that all schools will have trained and experienced SEN staff.
- Section Four is concerned with the criteria for making state-

ments of Special Educational Need, and refers to the relevant
and available provision.
- Section Five is concerned with assessment and statements for
  children under five.

It is important that a Head of a subject department knows the outline of
the Code of Practice and understands how it might affect those with whom
the department works. This is the legal basis for Special Educational Needs
provision. However, the detailed understanding and interpretation will be
the responsibility of the Head of Special Educational Needs (or their
equivalent), and a member of the Senior Management Team. It is therefore
necessary for the subject team to work closely with these people when the
team is addressing curriculum matters. The legal explanations may come
from colleagues, but the underlying expectations of access for all to the
curriculum must be led by the Head of Department.

Managing inspections and OFSTED visits

> The Education (Schools) Act 1992 significantly transformed the mode of school
> inspection. It replaced Her Majesty's Inspectorate (HMI), a small body of pro-
> fessionally independent inspectors, established in 1839, with HMCI/OFSTED. The
> responsibility for school inspections was thus assumed by privatised inspection teams
> contracted from the centre, guided by a framework document and overseen by a
> small number of HMIs.
>
> (Fitz and Lee, 1996 in Ouston, Earley and Fidler (eds), 1996, p. 10)

The nature of school inspections changed in the early 1990s from HMI
inspections which were run by highly trained and perceptive inspectors
whose task it was to inspect schools rigorously and also at times to act as
critical friend to schoolteachers (although offering less advice and support
and more distance and objectivity than Local Authority Inspectors). The
information gathered on inspections had an effect on national educational
policy and on pedagogy in general. In effect, the relationship was two-way –
schools that were inspected were given a clear view of their performance in
learning and teaching, and the issues raised by schools were fed back to
inform education in the future.

Janet Maw (1996), in the same book as Fitz and Lee (Ouston, Earley and
Fidler, 1996), writes about the new relationship between the inspection team
and the school as one of 'hierarchy and detachment'. She places teachers as
controlled and detached by the process to such an extent that they appear to
have no voice in the dialogue at all. It seems now that schools are usually
observed and measured during an OFSTED inspection – it is something that
is done to them – and the outcomes will not have any effect on education in
general in the future, unlike former HMI inspections. The relationship has
now become one-way.

OFSTED published the *Handbook for the Inspection of Schools* containing the
framework for inspections which tells inspectors what to inspect. Schools

originally invested in the Handbook in order to understand better what it was that was going to be examined. And indeed, several headteachers have taken part in the OFSTED training in order to 'know their enemy' and to understand better the criteria by which their schools are to be judged. So, gradually the inspection framework, addressed initially to inspectors, has been used by schools to plan their learning and teaching. They hope to make sure that when they are inspected, they will be seen to be 'doing it right'.

There is another perceived drawback with the OFSTED inspection procedure: the Inspection Framework section of *Handbook for the Inspection of Schools* seems to be taking the place of many schools' own development and curriculum planning. Thus, in much the same way that the National Curriculum is narrowing the interpretation of 'curriculum', the Handbook seems to be restricting the activities of schools because it is used as a constrictive framework: as a guideline for development planning. And even after being inspected, some schools find that the action plan they are required to draw up as a consequence of their inspection fits awkwardly with their previous development plans.

The introduction to this section might seem to be full of doom, gloom and despondency. But it is to show the backdrop to OFSTED inspections before which Heads of Department can continue to plan in ways based on their departmental educational principles. An understanding of the external context clarifies how team leaders need to manage internally in order to import their own values into the inspection process.

One note of optimism about OFSTED inspections is that among the first pieces of research on the process in English secondary schools were three studies done by Janet Ouston, Brian Fidler and Peter Earley, and published in the book they edited in 1996 (Ouston, Earley and Fidler, 1996). They showed that the vast majority of the headteachers they questioned were positive about the contribution that the process had made to the development of their schools.

However, they added some significant advice for those people who have management responsibilities in schools:

> Research work currently being undertaken at Oxford Brookes University suggests that classroom teachers, at least initially, may be less positive and even rather demoralised by the process. From informal discussion with schools, many report a period of 'post-inspection blues' at the end of the inspection, but this may become lessened as the findings become integrated with the school's work.
>
> (Ouston, Earley and Fidler, 1996, p. 120)

Nicola Brimblecombe, Michael Ormston and Marian Shaw, in a chapter in the same book, write that they found that more senior members of staff are probably less anxious about OFSTED inspections than classroom teachers. This appears to be because senior teachers tended to be heavily involved in the process from the start, so that they have a stronger sense of ownership of it than was felt elsewhere in the school (p. 129). This is another management issue – how can Heads of Department involve teachers more in planning for inspections without drowning them in paperwork?

Managing the paperwork is a key issue for Heads of Department involved in the OFSTED process. When talking to teachers on our courses, it became clear that those who work in schools where there are effective and useful paperwork systems already in place as an integral part of managing the school have found preparation for inspection less onerous and traumatic. Suggested Activity 25 may help reassure Heads of Department about necessary paperwork in preparing for an OFSTED inspection.

Suggested Activity 25

This discussion is for either the Head of Department and the second in charge of the department, or for the whole team together:

In the paperwork sent to a school which was about to be inspected at the end of 1995, the OFSTED team included the following schedule for inspection interview questions:

INTERVIEWS

A timetable for interviews will be set out before the inspection if possible. Inspectors will want to interview members of staff who have specific responsibilities, especially subject responsibilities. The interviews about subject responsibilities will usually focus on the following items:

- management of the subject
- resources and their management
- planning for pupils with different needs
- content of the curriculum
- arrangements for assessment, recording and reporting
- standards of achievement of pupils

Evidence available may include:
- exam results/NC assessment/teacher assessment
- samples of work
- teacher plans and records
- curriculum plans, time allocation, guidelines, schemes of work
- resources including accommodation

What would you need to consider about the management of your area of curriculum responsibility when preparing to answer the questions in this interview schedule?

Most Heads of Department who read through this interview schedule will realize that they and their team members already have most of the necessary paperwork in hand. Those middle managers who have struggled and have worried about drowning under the weight of paper have often been those whose school philosophies of education were not at one with the educational aims of the OFSTED inspection. This is particularly clear, for example, when teachers are working in Special Schools for young people with emotional and behavioural disorders. Teachers most deeply involved in this work are concerned with the whole young person in their care, and are afraid that the OFSTED inspection will focus too closely on the National Curriculum content of their work. Their fears about the paperwork include their expectations that it will deflect them from what they see as the real aim of their work.

Thus, on the whole, in the mainstream schools which serve the vast majority of the school population, the questions asked and the paperwork demanded by OFSTED teams are those which underpin good curriculum planning practice. Those teachers who see themselves engaged in work in which curriculum planning is less important than intensive interactions with individual young people think that they have more to fear, or more to argue with when they are given their action points at the end of an inspection.

Many experienced headteachers and senior managers in schools, when talking about their experiences of 'being OFSTEDed', advise staff in schools which are to be inspected to develop a sense of ownership about the process, in order to understand fully the procedure, but also so that there is some room for negotiation during the actual process. In this way, they see the process as becoming more two-way, and so they hope to have more influence on the outcomes and on the judgements made about their schools. However, as a middle manager, it is necessary to think about the research quoted previously – how can you and you team develop some ownership in the process?

Here is a summary of some points about the OFSTED procedure:

- Although the main changes in the inspection procedure began in the early 1990s, educationists took some time to 'read' and make sense of what was happening. In other words, definitions of and research about the effects of OFSTED inspections were really only beginning to be published in the late 1990s. This meant that there was and still is a sense of the unknown about the procedure, which has leant it an air of mystery and some fear (especially when it became linked with the nomination of good and bad teachers).
- There are very specific management issues about information within the process – it is important to involve the whole team in the process so that they know what is happening, without over-burdening them with unnecessary paperwork.
- If the paperwork that a subject team regularly completes is agreed to be worthwhile by everyone in the team, and is seen as an effective way of monitoring the curriculum in the subject area,

it is likely that the team will not have to do large amounts of extra paperwork for the inspection.

- The team must know and understand where the *Framework for Inspection* impacts on the specific subject area, but at the same time the team leader must try to keep a wider perspective on all their curriculum responsibilities.

Knowing how the curriculum area is taught

Some teachers believe that the only way a Head of Department can *really* know how the other members of the team teach is by entering their classroom. There are several other indicators, and a perceptive team leader pays attention to all possible indicators in order to know that good work is going on. These may include:

- discussions about teaching methods
- sharing materials
- looking over lesson plans
- reviewing attainment targets
- collaborative planning sessions
- and team teaching.

An agreed formal visit to a classroom while a lesson is taking place, flanked by discussions with the teacher before and after the visit, could be a very productive way for both adults concerned. But classroom observation is a complicated issue, and should not be undertaken lightly.

Beginning teachers and newly qualified teachers are used to classroom visitors, but some long-established teachers still have conflicting and complicated views about their 'privacy' when teaching in their own classroom. There has long been a debate among teachers around the definition of 'professionalism'. This debate is often based on teachers and their autonomy in choosing what they actually do in the classroom. Writing in the sociology of education referred to the Black Box – the formerly unresearched void that was the classroom behind closed doors, inhabited by teachers and young people. There is now a great deal of research and writing about what actually happens in the classroom, and the National Curriculum and the OFSTED procedure have made it essential that there should be discussions in schools about the actual activity of teaching. Indeed, the GEST accredited courses for primary curriculum coordinators must include some time spent on either classroom observation or other ways of ascertaining what is going on in the classroom with reference to coordinators' curriculum responsibility.

But there is still a vestigial resistance in some older teachers to being observed by their colleagues, especially if the colleague (or Head of Department) is younger and more senior, but is less experienced in teaching. Sometimes this resistance is based on insecurity, sometimes it is linked with a mistrust of new ideas and of energetic managers, and sometimes it is

founded on a mistrust of and disagreement with the fundamental philosophy of the National Curriculum and OFSTED. It is necessary to try to
understand the basis for the resistance, because different causes require
different ways of working with them.

As the probable appraiser of members of the department, the Head of
Department will be aware that the appraisal process includes a carefully set
up classroom observation, in which negotiation about the actual activity to
be observed depends on an equal balance of power between the appraiser
and the appraisee. And basic understandings about power and equity should
be remembered whenever a classroom visit is planned. In this way formal
classroom observation becomes an activity which is clearly agreed by everyone involved, although it might still make teachers nervous and
uncomfortable. Nevertheless, when it is done properly, there will be no
hidden agendas.

Many managers recommend informal visits, sometimes on other pretexts,
to see what is really going on in the classroom. Informal visits are easier and
less nerve-racking for teachers, but they can be complicated by hidden
agendas. Teachers may be given mixed messages: 'I am just dropping in
informally, *but*, I am making judgements about your work without proper
discussion with you.' If members of a departmental team regularly enter
each others' classrooms while teaching is going on, and regularly talk about
their work together, and if they have an atmosphere of trust and expectations of the best from each other, then informal visits cannot be
misinterpreted. But if a team leader's 'drop-in session' is really a way of
monitoring teaching without admitting to it, it will be almost impossible to
use the evidence gathered in a helpful and constructive way.

Primary teachers are much more comfortable about being seen while
teaching because they know that discussion about teaching methods can
encourage trust and collegiality in team members. There are some suggestions from primary schools which can be transferred productively if a Head
of Department meets with resistance from colleagues. These suggestions are
based on principles which go to build sound teamwork, and so will seem
familiar to those who have read the earlier chapters in this book about
working with teams.

- Team leaders have a responsibility for working at developing an
  ethos of trust and information in the team.
- One way of sharing ideas is that team meetings could regularly
  have a space where five minutes is spent on 'ideas about teaching'. Here, team members could bring examples of good or new
  practice, or might present a problem for the whole team to work
  through together. This session would encourage reflection on
  teaching, and would ensure that the discussion would remain
  non-judgemental.
- An acceptance that classroom visits are important necessitates a

decision about whether it is absolutely necessary to arrange formal observation sessions, or whether the ethos of the team encourages informal visits from each other, but with a clear understanding that the visits are non-judgemental.

- It is necessary to agree that the classroom observation is not about doing it the right way or doing it the wrong way – it is more about what can be learnt from each other, and what learning can come from mistakes.
- If team members agree to encourage regular visits to each others' classrooms so that the team can observe each other teaching, it may be helpful to begin by welcoming them into the team leader's own lessons, especially the team members who feel awkward about having the Head of Department in their classes. This invitation could come early in the whole process of watching each other teach.
- Team teaching is an excellent way of both seeing each other teach, and sharing the burden of planning for difficult work. It can take place either in colleagues' classrooms or the team leader's own, as long as everyone remains while each team member is teaching.
- A team that works well together and respects all its members will be comfortable with an informality which includes slipping into and out of each others' classrooms, and everyone will share responsibility for teaching the curriculum area well.

Evaluating the curriculum area

The study of evaluation and the techniques of evaluation became a fast growing area of scholarship at the end of the 1980s. Teachers initially divided the field into **summative** and **formative** evaluation.

Summative evaluation is more like assessment in that it summarizes and measures what has been learnt, and is a way of judging the perceived success of teaching of the curriculum – for example, examinations and Standard Assessment Tests (SATs). It is often quickly done, like marking examinations, and is about getting 'it' right or wrong. Summative evaluation tells people where they have got up to, is easily quantifiable, and can be used for comparative statistics such as league tables. Students' work is usually assessed in this way, but the league tables and results which describe these results are also used as a way of evaluating the work of departments in schools.

Formative evaluation is that which is concerned with giving ongoing information in order to reflect on and improve the process of learning and teaching as it is happening. It is more interactive than summative evaluation, and happens during rather than at the end of an activity. It is part of the learning process itself, and is one of the ways by which teachers can learn as well. Formative evaluation happens continuously in a learning school. It is part of the productive discussion between learners and teachers, but it is often non-verbal and apparent in the body language of learners – in their enthusiasm and curiosity, or in their boredom and disturbing behaviour. At its best and most effective, it helps learners reflect on what they have learnt and what they still need to learn as well as letting teachers know how and what they have taught. However, formative evaluations are difficult to measure and to compare with each other, they take time to complete, and are often more impressionistic than summative evaluations.

This is a summary of two styles of evaluation. It is not as nuanced as the many different ways that experienced teachers have of evaluating their work. But it does underline and explain the resistances and problems for teachers who saw evaluation as part of the (formative) learning process, and then became legally bound to do much more measured (summative) evaluation and testing of their teaching.

I am ashamed to say that when I was teaching in school and a colleague suggested that we should all evaluate our work, my first reaction was to say, most unkindly, that she must have just returned from attendance on a course. I saw evaluation then as only summative and instrumental, and something that I scarcely did apart from during exams. I did not recognize that my attempts – to involve the young people with whom I worked in reflection on their own learning as an important and integral part of the learning and teaching process – were clearly types of formative evaluation.

On reflection, I do not know how I could have decided whether my teaching was 'working'. I usually knew impressionistically when it was, and was good at reading non-verbal communication in my classroom. But I had no theoretical framework and no philosophical understanding about how I was checking my work, or even that I *was* checking my teaching, so it was unsystematic and fairly haphazard. And I missed out on the most important aspect of it all – really understanding the opportunity good evaluation procedures bring to both learners and teachers to talk about learning and teaching in a way that is not judgemental and that may be very constructive.

There are some very basic questions about evaluating teaching and learning that a departmental team could answer together. The answers to these questions should open up and develop the debate begun above. It is important that the questions are asked and answered in the order shown in Suggested Activity 26, because of the way they link with each other and because of their affect on the answers to the succeeding questions.

Answering these questions will help a department team consider the following:

- whether the learning the team is planning for 'works' at least as well as they intend it to;
- whether there is any room for improvement and what form that improvement might take;
- whether the methods they employ of assessing their teaching are effective and the most appropriate methods for their needs.

Suggested Activity 26

Work with your whole team on this activity, in order to explore as much as you can together about evaluating your work.

Set up a flipchart with one of the following questions at the top of each of five consecutive pages, keeping the questions in the order below. Brainstorm each question, then before turning over the page to the next question, talk about the issues that each question raised.

1   What is evaluation?
2   Why evaluate?
3   What should be evaluated?
4   What are the difficulties when evaluating?
5   Of which methods of evaluation are you aware?

It is important also to agree that teachers will do something useful with the outcomes of their different evaluation processes. Evaluation is only part of a cycle, not an end product in itself. It is only really worthwhile when it is closely and productively connected with learning and teaching.

In my present work, I cannot conceive of planning a repeat of a course until both tutors and participants have evaluated the learning and teaching – evaluation is now deeply embedded in all the work I do and it informs our planning for subsequent courses. But equally, we constantly engage in Brookfield's 'learning conversation' (Brookfield, 1993) with course participants during a course; we ask them for a summative evaluation (a form to complete on our teaching) at the very end of the course; and we send out a questionnaire six months after the end of a course which asks them to reflect on changes in their practice and whether we should change anything about ours. These are different forms of evaluation, using different processes and asking different questions at and about different stages of learning and teaching. But they all inform the planning of the next session of learning and teaching. They are all integral parts of the learning and teaching process which would be seriously diminished without them.

Managing constant change

Change is such a fundamental dynamic in educational management at the moment that the *management* of change is a rich area of academic writing and research, and it holds a central place in any course of advanced study about management. There is a tension between the drive for careful strategic planning in schools, and the acknowledgement that there is always change. Many schools operate superb planning strategies, consulting fully and effectively with their staff, and then external constraints impose the need to change the plans, quickly. A key management skill is the ability to make plans, then to alter them without losing the central concerns and main aims of the organization. It is important to be able to change plans without any sense of loss, and to continue to see change as opportunity.

The titles of books about managing education reflect the force and tumult discharged by the changes: Mike Wallace and Agnes McMahon wrote *Planning Change for Turbulent Times* in 1994, Andy Hargreaves wrote *Changing Times, Changing Teachers* the same year, Michael Fullan wrote *Change Forces* in 1993, and David Hargreaves and David Hopkins wrote *The Empowered School* in 1991. (See References section for further details relating to these books.)

There is certainly change in the external context of schooling. There are economic, political and sociological changes which are altering the shape of the world at the moment. There are fundamental changes within Britain which have reshaped the fabric of our society in the last twenty years; and there are political and educational changes which have reframed our definition of schooling.

Internally, too, people who work in schools have responded to external changes in different ways. Personal interactions are affected by strong emotions, especially when those involved feel threatened professionally. Teachers who have little sense of professional worth are going to be harder to motivate to plan changes, and successful change may be hard to recognize if people still feel unhappy. Strategies for managing change often leave little space for the messiness and incompleteness of many emotional interactions.

External changes have made an impact on the internal workings of schools, and most British schools have been involved in large numbers of changes all at the same time. Many educationists question the purpose of all of these changes, and I think that the root of my disquiet lies here: there is an optimum number of changes in which to be involved at any time, in order to perform well. Above that number, helplessness and eventually demoralization set in – and demoralized workers are easier to control because they do not rebel. So how can Heads of Departments work with externally imposed change while keeping their teams creative and effective?

Bolam and his colleagues (1993) found that although all the schools they looked at were suffering from 'innovation overload', some seemed to have coped better than others. They found that 'there was considerable agreement that too much was demanded too quickly' (p. 97). Maybe it is important to be involved in some change so that teachers do not become stultified and stagnant in their work. But when we ask teachers how many changes they are working with currently, they range from six to twelve! The majority of these changes are imposed from outside – so they are difficult for those internal to the school to manage within their own belief system and time frame.

Beryl Husain uses a paper about managing change which fits in here, and which goes further to explain some of the problems associated with constant and externally imposed change:

I   Generalisations about the change process
From evidence of research and experience it is possible to draw up some generalisations about the change process:
– change should be seen as a *process* which takes place within a social system context
– change is a *dynamic process* not an event
– various people, agents and systems involved in the change process interact with each other over time and are changed by the change experience itself
– an innovation should not be seen as unchangeable but should be regarded as something which is bound to change over time
– the implementation phase is the most crucial one in the whole process and must be carefully prepared and planned
– effective implementation will normally involve a process of mutual adaptation by change agents and members of target user group
– change engages both intellect and emotions – affects individuals as well as organisations – these factors must be taken into account
– there are always obstacles to change – some obvious, others latent

II   Characteristics of successful innovations
From the literature it appears that an innovation has much greater likelihood *of being successfully implemented* if it meets as many as possible of the following conditions:
– it should be centrally relevant to the members of the target user group
– it should bring major benefits to people as well as the organisation
– it should be simple and flexible
– its underlying values should be congruent with those of the target user group and those of the institution
– it should be feasible in terms of its costs and in its implications for individuals (e.g. status, work-load, etc.)

III   Successful implementation strategies
A successful implementation strategy will meet most of the following conditions:
– it should involve adaptive and continuing planning by the major participants and interest groups involved, giving an opportunity to adapt the goals and content of the innovation and providing mechanisms for feedback on progress
– people in key leadership roles should be overtly supportive and participate directly when appropriate

- staff training should be provided in a relevant and continuing form, should give specific and practical 'how to do it' information, where possible provided by peers and practitioners and where appropriate in an on-the-job setting
- continuing support should be provided and should be both practical and personal
- there should be opportunities for members of the target user group to develop and modify the innovation locally by adapting materials and by learning about the innovation's characteristics and developing a sense of 'owning' it
- a 'critical mass' of people involved should be developed so that individuals do not feel isolated but can meet together with like-minded enthusiasts as a team for discussion, information-sharing and training
- take into account the feelings, values, ideas and experience of others

IV   Characteristics of successful change organisations
Characteristics of the setting in which successful innovation occurs:
- purpose of institution clear
- change agent well-regarded by the members of the target user group and should, therefore, have the right status and authority, the right leadership style, and ideally, a successful 'track record' of innovation implementation
- the institution should itself be receptive to change, and should have high staff morale, and the active support and commitment of the head of the institution or department
- the organisation or system members should also be adaptive and thus ready to change structures, timetables and role behaviours within the various departments and sub-structures
- power to do things should be delegated to where needed, and process decisions made at the right level
- communications should be open and frank, with conflict managed constructively using problem solving methods
- individuals' identity, integrity and freedom respected, all members and their work valued
- all have a degree of autonomy within the disciplined framework of shared values

(Source: Beryl Husain, *Management of Change*, Management Development Centre Handout)

These suggestions all go to show that managers have the most important part to play in any change process. Change must be managed, should be planned for, but mainly it is necessary to believe in it so that it can be managed with integrity.

Reading curriculum legislation

It is not my intention to address specific curriculum documents here because the syllabus for each subject is defined in great detail in several official documents. I would like, however, to offer some observations about how to read those documents. Several writers about the policy of education have explored the way that a written policy can be 'read'. Richard Bowe, Stephen Ball and I explored the differences between 'readerly' and 'writerly' texts in *Reforming Education and Changing Schools* (Bowe, Ball and Gold, 1993). We used the work of Roland Barthes (cited in Hawkes, 1977) to distinguish between texts which are 'readerly', or in other words offer the minimum opportunity for creative interpretation by the reader; and those which are 'writerly' and which appear to invite the reader to interpret, to co-operate and almost to co-author.

Given that a government policy has legal weight behind it, it is usually written with the *intention* that it will make absolutely clear that which it sets out to enforce. Readers expect it to be written as carefully and unequivocally as possible, so that there can be virtually no room for ambiguity or interpretation. But readers always interpret what is written. Even the simplest of texts, and those with no political intent, are open to a different representation by each reader. Do the readers of a text make the sense of it that the writer intended? Is their reading of a text informed by their cultural, sociological and educational beliefs and understandings? Is their reading of a text a form of intepretation of it? Suggested Activity 27 offers some questions to answer about reading policy documents.

Suggested Activity 27

This is a particularly important set of questions when thinking about how to read government educational policy documents. As a Head of Department who is reading policy documents to inform your curriculum planning:

- Do you read them as a direct and exacting set of rules to be obeyed?
- Do you filter what you read through your beliefs about education, and attempt to make it match or fit?
- Or do you read for loopholes and for spaces for different interpretations than those intended?

Unconsciously, there are always different interpretations of written words. Consciously, those who wish to find ways of resisting that of which they disapprove, usually read very carefully, searching for a way round the rules. And policy writers are quite aware that people who read their texts do so looking for ways of resisting or interpreting what they mean. Such writers are carefully trained to write as unambiguously as possible.

> Policy authors do make concerted efforts to assert control by the means at their disposal, to achieve a 'correct' reading. We need to understand those efforts and their effects on readers and to recognize the attention that readers pay to the writers' context of production and communicative intent. But in addition, it is crucial to recognize that the policies themselves, the texts, are not necessarily clear or closed or complete.
>
> (Ball, 1994, p. 16)

It is for that lack of clarity, closedness or completeness that those who wish to resist policies search while reading official guidance papers.

I realize that I have written about what might be interpreted as a deliberate act of sabotage. Not all readings of policy documents may be so instrumental or resistant. But it is almost impossible to manage what one does not agree with. In other words, it is necessary for a team leader to read a document to find ways of being able to agree with it and to see how worthwhile it is before they can work with their team to implement changes that chime in with their beliefs.

Conclusion

If you read this book in order to decide whether to become a Head of Department, I hope you have found an answer: it can be an exciting, creative, exhausting and centrally important job. But do not drift into it, or take it on because you think you *should*, or because it *ought* to be the next stage in your career. It really is professionally acceptable to remain a classroom teacher working directly with young people and concentrating on learning and teaching at first hand. All schools need excellent teachers whose principal responsibility is classroom teaching, and young people and beginning teachers need to see more mature teachers spending their time in the classroom. This was recognized by the decision to pay classroom teachers more, by the creation of the group known as Expert Teachers, and by the teacher grading system employed by OFSTED. It is important that people who choose to become Heads of Department are as comfortable working with other adults to plan the teaching and learning as they are working with young people to deliver it in the classroom.

But if you are already a Head of Department, or have decided to become one, enjoy the stimulation, the challenge and the possibilities! The role is a pivotal one, making and informing decisions about learning and teaching in schools, and making sure that those decisions are put into practice. The requisite skills are a collection of knowledge-based and people-based capacities, most of which can be developed as long as the reasons for their development are clear.

Most important, however, is the articulation of a set of educational principles which underpin management practice. Many educators have different principles, but ensuring that all management actions are informed by principles must be the most significant one. Several management strategies are suggested in this book as ways of finding enough time and space to be able to get in touch with those fundamental principles. And managers are asked to encourage the rest of their team to talk about their educational principles together.

Another overarching principle is the one which allows managers to understand notions of power, and which encourages them to wish to address issues of power 'in order to', rather than power 'over'. This understanding affects the way Heads of Departments work with their teams. It informs the way they talk and listen to their team members, and it influences the attention they give to encouraging members of their department to develop professionally. In an external ethos of competition and rivalry, this principle encourages teachers to model collaboration and attempts to achieve consensus, and reminds managers to ensure that all members of the team have a voice.

The knowledge base relevant for a Head of Department is not just about a subject or curriculum area. There are legal responsibilities for the management of special educational needs, and relevant knowledge of good employment practice which influences selection and recruitment procedures. Knowledge about budgeting strategies and procedures and an understanding of local financial management is encouraged (and ways to do so or to get help from others who know how to do so, are suggested).

Good interpersonal skills are highly relevant for Heads of Department. Theories about adult learning are described, in order to inform the way people work together, and an effective Head of Department pays a great deal of attention to acquiring effective interpersonal skills. Working with other people is the most creative interaction, one which requires care and thought and planning. Strategies are offered to find ways of developing objectivity, especially when strong feelings such as conflict threaten to cloud important issues.

Indeed, many times in this book, the reader is encouraged to find ways of striking a balance between responding to other people's crises, dealing with the heavy demands of daily school life, and exploring strategies to be a reflective manager. An effective middle manager eventually manages to juggle all these demands, and to plan for the future!

References

Adair, J. (1986) *Effective Teambuilding*. London: Pan.

Armstrong, L. (1993) *Managing to Survive: A Guide for Middle Managers in Secondary Schools. Volume I – Organisation*. Lancaster: Framework Press.

Ball, S. J. (1990) *Foucault and Education*. London: Routledge.

Ball, S. J. (1994) *Education Reform: A Critical and Post-structural Approach*. Buckingham: Open University Press.

Belbin, R. Meredith (1981) *Management Teams*. Oxford: Heinemann.

Belbin, R. Meredith (1993) *Team Roles at Work*. Oxford: Butterworth-Heinemann.

Bell, L. (1992) *Managing Teams in Secondary School*. London: Routledge.

Bion, W. R. (1961) *Experiences in Groups*. London: Tavistock.

Bolam, R., MacMahon, A., Pocklington, K. and Weindling, R. (1993) *Effective Management in Schools*. London: HMSO.

Bottery, M. (1992) *The Ethics of Educational Management*. London: Cassell.

Bowe, R. and Ball, S. J. with Gold, A. (1993) *Reforming Education and Changing Schools*. London: Routledge.

Bowles, S. and Gintis, H. (1976) *Schooling in Capitalist America*. London: Routledge.

Brimblecome, N., Ormston, M. and Shaw, M. (1996) 'Teachers' perceptions of inspections', in Ouston, J., Earley, P. and Fidler, B. (eds) *OFSTED Inspections: The Early Experience*. London: David Fulton.

Brookfield, S. A. (1993) *Developing Critical Thinkers*. Milton Keynes: Open University Press.

Devlin, T. and Knight, B. (1990) *Public Relations and Marketing for Schools*. Harlow: Longman.

DFE (1994) *Code of Practice on the Identification and Assessment of Special Educational Needs*. London: HMSO.

DfEE (1994) *School Governors – A Guide to the Law*. London: DfEE

Fish, J. and Evans, J. (1995) *Managing Special Education*. Buckingham: Open University Press.

Fitz, J. and Lee, J. (1996) 'Where angels fear', in Ouston, J., Earley, P. and

Fidler, B. (eds) *OFSTED Inspections: The Early Experience.* London: David Fulton.

Fullan, M. (1993) *Change Forces.* London: Falmer Press.

Gewirtz, S., Ball, S. and Bowe, R. (1995) *Markets, Choice and Equity in Education.* Buckingham: Open University Press.

Grace, G. (1995) *School Leadership: Beyond Education Management.* London: Falmer Press.

Hall, V. (1996) *Dancing on the Ceiling: A Study of Women Managers in Education.* London: Paul Chapman Publishing.

Hargreaves, A. (1994) *Changing Times, Changing Teachers.* London: Cassell.

Hargreaves, D. and Hopkins, D. (1991) *The Empowered School.* London: Cassell.

Hart, J. (1993) *Successful Financial Planning and Management of Schools.* Harlow: Longman.

Hawkes, T. (1977) *Structuralism and Semiotics.* London: Methuen.

Ironside, M. and Seifert, R. (1995) *Industrial Relations in Schools.* London: Routledge.

Jaques, D. (1991) *Learning in Groups.* London: Kogan Page.

Kolb, D. (1984) *Experiential Learning.* New Jersey: Prentice Hall.

McCormick, R. and James, M. (1983) *Curriculum Evaluation in Schools.* London: Routledge.

Marland, M. (1986) *School Management Skills.* Oxford: Heinemann.

Marland, M. and Rogers, R. (1991) *Marketing the School.* Oxford: Heinemann.

Maw, J. (1996) 'The handbook for inspection of schools: models, outcomes and effects', in Ouston, J., Earley, R. and Fidler, B. (eds) *OFSTED Inspections: The Early Experience.* London: David Fulton.

Ouston, J., Earley, P. and Fidler, B. (eds) (1996) *OFSTED Inspections: The Early Experience.* London: David Fulton.

Sayer, J. (1989) *Managing Schools.* London: Hodder & Stoughton.

Sayer, J. (1993) *The Future Governance of Education.* London: Cassell.

Schön, D. A. (1987) *Educating the Reflective Practitioner.* San Francisco: Jossey-Bass.

Torrington, D. and Weightman, J. (1989) *The Reality of School Management.* Oxford: Blackwell.

Wallace, M. and MacMahon, A. (1994) *Planning Change for Turbulent Times.* London: Cassell.

Whitty, G. (1985) *Sociology and School Knowledge.* London: Methuen.

Willis, P. (1977) *Learning to Labour.* Farnborough: Gower.

Wragg, E. C. (1987) *Teacher Appraisal: A Practical Guide.* Basingstoke: Macmillan.

Wragg, E. C. (1994) 'A national survey of teacher appraisal, 1992–4: a preliminary analysis.' Paper presented at the annual conference of the British Educational Research Association, Oxford, September 1994.

Yule, W. and Gold, A. (1993) *Wise Before the Event: Coping with Crises in Schools.* London: Gulbenkian Foundation.

Index